ENDORSEMENTS

Donna Reiners is a proven author and an anointed teacher. She's also a committed practitioner who diligently helps individuals overcome myriads of diverse circumstances. By the end of this 40-day study, you will have the answers that empower you with increased momentum towards the fulfillment of your life goals.

Rev. Jill Mitchell O'Brien
President, Kingdom Connections International Inc.
kingdom-connections.com

I met Donna Reiners in 2014, and from the start I knew this lady was not normal. The Word tells us we are a peculiar people and that we are to be different. We are to stand out and not do things the way the world does them. We are to be set apart. Donna has done a great job in writing this book to help you do that very thing. She has laid out some principles that give you a great foundation on how to build according to God's way and not the world's way of doing things. As her pastor, I can say that Donna's greatest attribute is that she truly loves people and wants to help them find the Source from where this Love originates. I pray you enjoy this book but most of all, I hope you find the love of the Father. I hope you feel the passion that Donna carries to know Him and to make Him known.

Darrin Begley
Author, *I AM identified*
Pastor, God's House, Inc.
godshouse.life
Branded By God Ministries
brandedbygod.com

Attention: This may well be the most significant and transformational book you have read in your whole life. Read it carefully, slowly and dutifully. You owe this to yourself. This is also a daring book in that it plunges us into the massive flock of problems that gather around our dealing with our concepts of self. Let's face it, we have a tendency to think either too much or too little of ourselves because self is always with us. What a novel idea, to avoid both these dangerous pitfalls by intentionally agreeing with God and loving ourselves. This book walks in "where angels fear to tread."

The author has dared from the beginning to open the curtains on her past, the trials, the failures, the battles, the inner demons and all. She has emerged from her past, not only with a limp but also to an enlightened life of God's love. I love her "synopses", beyond a dozen, that form the foundations of truth from which she writes and speaks. I also love the challenges issued in her demands of openness and

I've known Donna Reiners for well over two decades. The consistent and unwavering passion for the Lord and His purposes in her life has been evident and contagious to all those around her. Writing skills are a gift that can be developed and honed; yet she brings revelation and relevance to her gifts through her own life lessons and life experiences. In her latest book, *40 Days to the BRAVE New You: Love Yourself Without Limits*, Donna uniquely ties together some important points and the understanding of The Hope of Glory, Christ in you, thus the understanding of who you are in Christ. The honesty and candor, in which Donna integrates crucibles of experience with scarlet threads of redemption, hope, encouragement, and purpose is quite intriguing and refreshing.

Doug Stringer
Founder/President, Somebody Cares &
Turning Point Ministries
dougstringer.com

Prepare to be impacted by *40 Days to the BRAVE New You: Love Yourself Without Limits*! I have known Donna Reiners for 25 years and have seen how she has devoted her life to knowing the Truth of God's word; faithful intercession and helping scores of people get healed, delivered and set free. This devotional is not another self-help book, but an intentional relationship-builder with Jesus. What

honesty on all our parts. She invites, yea, demands us to take the truth into our *minds* and think it, then speak it with our *mouths* and, most important of all, activate it into a lifestyle of *movement*.

I thrill at the possibility of this becoming a text for study with individuals, small groups, large groups, old groups and young groups. Thanks, Donna for opening your life to us in daring and stunning vulnerability! I predict for this treatise a fantastic future!

Jack Taylor
President, Dimensions Ministries
Melbourne, Florida
jackrtaylor.com

I have known Donna Reiners for over 20 years. She has been a forerunner in mentorship and in the ministry of intercession. As a coach she has inspired many men and women to reach the heights of potential within their lives. I highly recommend *40 Days to the BRAVE New You: Love Yourself Without Limits*. This book will inspire the reader to reach the endless possibilities, which God has afforded them.

Lenny Weston
Founder, Vision Ministries International
Senior Pastor, Bridge Church Columbus
thebridgechurchcolumbus.com

could be more important than setting aside time to know Jesus Christ more deeply and be known by Him? You will find a daily feast on the Person of Truth while addressing deep questions to affirm your value, bring healing and build you up in God's Love!

I believe your heart will be changed as you go through this book. As you begin to see yourself by the Spirit you will step into a fresh value for yourself. You will learn to love yourself, understand your worth in Christ and deepen your love for God. This will positively affect your relationships, families and communities for the glory of God.

Bethany Martin
Songwriter/Recording Artist, MaryofBethany.com
Director, Heart of Texas House of Prayer
heartoftexashouseofprayer.com
State Ambassador — Texas, Awaken The Dawn

PRAISE FROM READERS

"After life threw a series of tough blows, I felt depleted and overwhelmed. I earnestly prayed, 'God, You are my Source. Please send resources to help me.' An answer came with '40 Days to the BRAVE New You'. Every time I opened a new topic, it applied to the very moment I was in. Not only did I find much healing and truth, I was also reminded who I am and inspired to have joy in a fresh perspective. I am taking more risks and finding adventure as I learn to stay out of a box, believing in myself with grace and kindness. We are created to know Love. This book will encourage you to hear His voice and appreciate yours. We can change the world by starting with ourselves and living fully. I am liking the freer, truer edition of myself. I bless you to know everlasting hope and to embrace the real you too."

—Jennifer Greagrey, Texas

"I remember a day when I was sitting outside and going through the lesson of the day. I felt such a real closeness and oneness with the Lord. I remember sitting there just weeping — not a sad weeping — but a cleansing and it was so sweet. Also, when I went through it I had an accountability partner and it really helped me build some good habits in seeking God, reading the Word and talking about issues. I would do it again."

—Adele, Texas

"The first day I had a very interesting leadership thing happen. While in a department head meeting we had to make some tough decisions to terminate a few folks for lack of performance. We took our time and did the normal strength vs. weaknesses comparisons. When we finished up (2 hours) later we all went to lunch and the three department heads asked me to say Grace over lunch. I have been here for 5.5 years and that has never happened. GOD is at work. I'm in day 3 and have been thoughtful, about myself, and those around me, not an unusual thing. I like the hold your hand thing which, I hadn't thought of before. Therapeutic and self-aware gesture to be sure."

—Greg, Texas

"I am so thankful for Donna Reiners and for this transformational book. Donna has a beautiful spirit and the heart of God flowing through all she does. She has a deep passion to share God's love and the powerful impact it has on people's lives when they feel that love — for real. Her faith and wisdom have deeply inspired me. Donna helps to reveal the oft-hidden middle step between loving God and loving others is learning to love YOU. I know her words will help many people to find their strength in Christ, begin loving themselves, and living their best lives — bravely, boldly, with courage, compassion, and joy.

In October 2017, I worked with Donna as she did a Christ-centered emotional healing session with me that helped release a deep wound and helped me accept Jesus into my heart. I will forever be grateful to her for *taking that time with me. The insight and power of her prayers in the Holy Spirit are stunning in their depth, thoroughness, and beauty. You see those at work in this book as well. I am confident that '40 Days to the BRAVE New You' will inspire many to love God, and truly love themselves and others the way God intended."*

—Jane VanVooren Rogers, Illinois

40 DAYS TO THE BRAVE NEW YOU

Love Yourself Without Limits

40 Days to the Brave New You:
Love Yourself Without Limits

By Donna Reiners

E-Books available on Amazon:

    Woman, Come Out of the Cave

    Voices in My Head

    Becoming One

    Fast and Pray for the Next Generation

    Talking Back to God (Respondiéndole a DIOS)

Follow @donnareiners @bravetobraver
on Instagram & Twitter & Facebook

40 DAYS TO THE BRAVE NEW YOU

Love Yourself Without Limits

Donna Reiners

40 Days to the BRAVE New You: Love Yourself Without Limits
Copyright © 2011 – 2018 Donna Reiners All rights reserved.
Paperback ISBN: 978-1-64085-308-9
Hardback ISBN: 978-1-64085-309-6
Library of Congress Control Number: 2018943187
SEL023000 Self-Help/Personal Growth/Self-Esteem
Printed in the United States of America
Published by Author Academy Elite
P. O. Box 43, Powell, OH 43055
www.AuthorAcademyElite.com

All rights reserved. This book is protected by the copyright laws of the United States of America. This book may not be copied or reprinted for commerce (gain or profit). For example, electronic, photocopy, recording — without the prior written permission of the publisher. The only exception is brief quotations in printed reviews.

Thanks to the following paid editors for this project:
Jane VanVooren & Jennifer Greagrey
Thanks to the paid designer who created the cover design for this project: Imran Shaikh (Retina99) retinaaa99@gmail.com - whom you can reach at retina99.com
Thanks to Chelsea Reiners who created the inside image designs - chelseathedesigner@gmail.com
All intellectual rights for names, companies, ideas, and graphics are owned by Donna and/or Craig Reiners and are intellectual property of Donna and/or Craig Reiners. All copyrights and/or trademarks are property of Donna Reiners and/or Craig Reiners.
"Scripture quotation taken from the New American Standard Bible (NASB), Copyright ©1960, 1962, 1963, 1968, 1971, 1972, 1973, 1975, 1977, 1995 by The Lockman Foundation. Al rights reserved." www.lockman.org
"Scripture Quotation marked NLT is taken from the Holy Bible, New Living Translation copyright 1996, 2004, 2015 by Tyndale House Foundation. Used by permission of Tyndale House Publishers, Inc. Carol Stream, Illinois, 60188 All Rights Reserved." www.tyndale.com
"Scripture quotations are from the ESV Bible (The Holy Bible, English Standard Version®), copyright © 2001 by Crossway, a publishing ministry of Good News Publishers. Used by permission. All rights reserved." www.crossway.org
"Scripture quotations taken from the Amplified® Bible (AMP), Copyright ©2015 by The Lockman Foundation Used by permission.www.Lockman.org"

"Scripture quotations marked TPT are from The Passion Translation®. Copyright ©2017 by Broadstreet Publisher® Group, LLC. Used by permission. All rights reserved. The PassionTranslation.com www.broadstreetpublishing.com

"Unless otherwise indicated, all Scripture quotations are taken from THE MESSAGE, Copyright © 1993, 1994, 1995, 1996, 2000, 2001, 2002 by Eugene H. Peterson. Used by permission of NavPress. All rights reserved. Represented by Tyndale House Publishers, Inc." www.navpress.com

"Biblesoft's New Exhaustive Strong's Numbers and Concordance with Expanded Greek-Hebrew Dictionary."

"The Voice Scripture taken from The Voice™. Copyright ©2012 by Ecclesia Bible Society. Used by permission. All rights reserved. www.harpercollinschristian.com."

Oftentimes, what appears to be a Scripture is a thought or an idea. Donna studied the *Amplified Bible* for years, and many times that is what comes from her mind and mouth. Other notes and ideas are created and/or written by Donna Reiners.

TO MY FAMILY

I thank my sisters for believing in me when I did not believe in me. Your strength and steadfast trust has been a rock for me in times I wanted to quit and stop writing altogether. I am thankful to know you and be in relationship with you for a lifetime. *I thank my niece and nephew* for continuing in relationship with us. You are both treasures. *I thank my husband* for believing in me. I love you. You have supported many projects and ideas. You are the most consistent and diligent person I know. I have learned confidence by watching you make decisions. I respect you more anyone I have ever known. You impress me every day with how you stay the course. Thank you for loving me and for embracing my family as your own.

DEDICATION

To Women Everywhere — I believe in you. If you struggle to love yourself, then this book is for you. I want you to know that though you have felt like you walk alone and that nobody understands — you are *not* alone and I *do* understand. I know what it is like not to like me — not to love me and not to believe in me. What a journey it has been to discover it is OK to love and believe in me.

One of my deepest desires is for you to believe in you too. Just be you, my friend; it is the only way to peace. You will find this book comforting and conversational. Mature believers have told me the content is very challenging because many have never loved themselves before, and many do not take time to know His love for them now. Allow Holy Spirit time to lead you into Love.

TABLE OF CONTENTS

ENDORSEMENTS 1
PRAISE FROM READERS 7
TO MY FAMILY 16
DEDICATION 17
TABLE OF CONTENTS 19
FOREWORD — BOB L. PHILLIPS 23
PREFACE 27

ACKNOWLEDGEMENTS 37

INTRODUCTION 39
BE GOOD — LOVE YOU 40
THIS IS ALL ABOUT YOU 41

PRAYING FOR YOU 43
OPTIONAL SMALL GROUPS 46

CHALLENGE 1   I AM LOVE 47
TEACHING — NAMELESS LOVE 48
LOVE YOURSELF LIST 60
DAY 1. WHAT IS LOVE? 62
DAY 2. I AM AT PEACE 64
DAY 3. CHRIST'S CONNECTION 66
DAY 4. LOVE LOOKS IN ON ME 68
DAY 5. I NEED OTHERS 71
LOVE TAKEAWAY 73

CHALLENGE 2   I AM BOLD 75
TEACHING — ARE YOU BOLD? 76
LOVE YOURSELF LIST 85

DAY 6. PETER 86
DAY 7. KILLER TO LOVER 89
DAY 8. GIRL TO MOTHER 91
DAY 9. SICK TO WHOLE 93
DAY 10. ADAM TO JESUS 96
BOLD TAKEAWAY 99

CHALLENGE 3 I AM RESPECT 101
TEACHING — RESPECT YOU? 102
LOVE YOURSELF LIST 110
DAY 11. LOVE IS PATIENT 112
DAY 12. FREE FROM GUILT 115
DAY 13. SPEAKING TRUTH 117
DAY 14. I VALUE MYSELF 120
DAY 15. I RESPECT MYSELF 122
RESPECT TAKEAWAY 124

CHALLENGE 4 I AM ACTIVATED 125
TEACHING — ARE YOU ACTIVATED? 126
LOVE YOURSELF LIST 135
DAY 16. GOD IS MY FRIEND 136
DAY 17. I TRUST GOD 138
DAY 18. I FIND HIS GOODNESS 140
DAY 19. I FOLLOW GOD 142
DAY 20. I AM SUCCESSFUL 144
ACTIVATED TAKEAWAY 146

CHALLENGE 5 I AM VICTORIOUS 147
TEACHING — VICTORIOUS PAST 148
LOVE YOURSELF LIST 160
DAY 21. GOD'S AFFIRMATION 161

DAY 22. ACCEPTING GOD'S LOVE 164
DAY 23. I AM THANKFUL 168
DAY 24. ACKNOWLEDGING JOY 170
DAY 25. GOD'S GOODNESS 173
VICTORIOUS TAKEAWAY 175

CHALLENGE 6   I AM ENCOURAGEMENT 177
TEACHING — ENCOURAGE YOU 178
LOVE YOURSELF LIST 180
DAY 26. MY PERSPECTIVE 181
DAY 27. GOD LIVES IN ME 183
DAY 28. HOW GOD SEES ME 185
DAY 29. I AM SALT 187
DAY 30. I FULFILL GOD'S PURPOSE 189
ENCOURAGEMENT TAKEAWAY 191

CHALLENGE 7   I AM HOPE 193
TEACHING — HOPE'S EYES 194
LOVE YOURSELF LIST 197
DAY 31. LOVE OF CHRIST 198
DAY 32. LIKENESS OF GOD 200
DAY 33. GOD LOVES ME 202
DAY 34. GOD GIVES ME LOVE 204
DAY 35. GOD'S TANGIBLE LOVE 206
HOPE TAKEAWAY 208

CHALLENGE 8   A BRAVE NEW ME 209
INTENTION — BRAVE NEW YOU 210
LOVE YOURSELF LIST 214
DAY 36. A BOLD NEW ME 216
DAY 37. A RESPECTFUL NEW ME 219

DAY 38. AN ACTIVATED NEW ME 225
DAY 39. A VICTORIOUS NEW ME 230
DAY 40. AN *IN-COURAGE* NEW ME 234
OUR TIME TOGETHER 238
BRAVE NEW FRIENDS 239
SMALL GROUP ADVENTURE 241
SMALL GROUP ASSIGNMENT 244
BRAVE NEW YOU TAKEAWAY 246

PRAYING FOR YOU **249**

RESOURCES AND THANK YOU **251**
BIOGRAPHY 253
ENDNOTES 255

FOREWORD — BOB L. PHILLIPS

If you don't know Donna Reiners, then you should. If you do know her, then immediately the thought of passion comes to mind — passion for Jesus and life. This series is a good course to get to know her and the One she is so passionate about: Jesus and His Presence.

In this series, laid out as practical challenges in a transforming journey, Donna becomes your thought provoker, your coach and mentor, and your encourager along the way. She will be a catalyst to a new you. You will be challenged to truly like yourself and provoked to a new boldness to become who God designed you to be. You know why? Because not only has God given her a revelation toward "a brave new you" she models the lifestyle by the way she lives.

Jesus came preaching a new kingdom — a kingdom of love like no one had ever seen. In the presence of Jesus' love, you will find treasures for yourself. Your life will revolutionize others around you. They will be grateful just to know you. Donna will not only give you revelations as to how to love anew, she will hold your hand and strengthen you along the way. Prepare to be challenged into a passionate relationship with Jesus. You are going to love the new you.

Bob L. Phillips
Bob L. Phillips Ministries, Inc.
Heartland Church in Ankeny, Iowa

Pastor Bob *moved to heaven April 20, 2017.* He married us — he was our spiritual father. He advised us when we were struggling. He encouraged me when I wanted to leave ministry. He was a source of strength and faith by how he lived his life. He responded to the bumps along the way with grace and integrity. He encouraged me to write and to reach into community to show the love of God to those who perhaps had given up on Him. Pastor Bob Phillips was a man of integrity, vision, strength, prayer and love.

We are honored he believed in us. We truly appreciated him. He and his wife Sherry were very kind to us through the years. One thing I watched in Pastor Bob through the years was how he imparted love and life to spiritual sons and daughters through every season of his life. What a rare man and rare gift of unconditional love to the body of Christ.

Pastor Bob was renowned globally as an apostolic father. Together with David Wilkerson, he was pastor of Times Square Church in New York City. Bob was a published author and ran a radio ministry, "Come Up Higher" for seven years. He started Hannah House, a home for unwed mothers. He served as Head of Pastoral Ministries and Chairman of the Board of the Brownsville School of Revival in Pensacola, Florida. For 15 years, he was pastor of Encourager Church, a thriving multi-cultural church located in Houston, Texas, where he also founded Kingdom School of Ministry. He was asked to speak at Oxford University twice, and at that time, as far as we know he had been the only Charismatic teacher to be invited. Pastor Bob served as the director of the Academy for Cultural Transformation, was one of the teaching pastors at Heartland Church, in Ankeny, Iowa and was part of the apostolic team for The Heartland Alliance.

Most importantly, he was a faithful husband who loved his wife and children unconditionally. He was a pastor who truly prayed and heard from God. He had a strong desire for others to have an intimate relationship with His Closest Companion, Jesus.

We know we will see him again.

PREFACE

I want to share some intimate things with you about my family. I share because I want to encourage you. I want you to know you are not alone. I want you to know you are loved. I want you to know others have faced similar tragedy, heartbreak and dysfunction as you. I want you to know that you too can overcome a history of poor decisions and a lifetime of false beliefs about yourself and others. My family history is part of the reason I have written *40 Days to the BRAVE New You*.

When I first came to know Father, He gave me a revelation of how the enemy had come to steal, kill and destroy the seed of life in our family. Let me explain.

He gave me a vision of my family tree that looked similar to a schematic. I'm going to be as forthcoming and straightforward as I can so you can get a clear picture of how it works in a family. At the same time, isn't real life just convoluted and complicated? Sometimes I think my life story is more interesting than daytime or nighttime soap operas. Let me share a bit of our relational dynamics and backgrounds. I am one of four daughters.

First, there was my oldest sister, whom at the time I did not know very well. Her past pain included being married to a man who suddenly left her after two decades of marriage. She had not worked outside the home enough to acquire a marketable skill. She was devastated and faced extremely difficult financial hardships for her entire lifetime. This sister did not come to know God personally until later in life when she turned from a strong religion to relationship with Him. Because of guilt and shame, she spent most of her life thinking very poorly of herself. Fast forward twenty years later when I became her caregiver and was with her as she moved from this planet into the heavens.

This oldest sister only had one child who was named after our mom. My niece is only about five years younger than myself, because my oldest sister was eighteen years older than me. My niece was the only grandchild my parents had through their children. She was not treated kindly and felt unloved throughout her childhood. She has a son who is my father's namesake. Her fight to find her value took her well into adulthood. She decided to give herself and her son new names. Why? Because her mother gave her our mom's name and she felt she needed a new name to define an identity without abuse. My niece has a special sense of humor and has lived a difficult life. She has been a good mom and has learned how to live life in a way many of us never experience. My niece also renamed her son — my nephew so he was also not identified by any abuse from her past. My nephew is brilliant and kind and protective of his mom. Although we did not really get to truly know one another until we were older, I am thankful for our relationships. They are blessings.

Then there is my next-to-oldest sister, who never married or had children. She was in love once many years ago, but her heart was broken, and she turned to food as her comforter. She was heavy for many years until a weight loss surgery. Sadly, the medical profession did not give clear instructions on nutrition. Eventually, we discovered she had a B vitamin deficiency so bad it could have killed her. Instead, it atrophied her brain and she suffers from short-term memory loss at the time of this writing. We are thankful she not only loves God but has refused to blame Him for the outcome of her life. She has persevered and has maintained her sense of humor and authenticity. Her love for God encourages me.

Finally, the sister born before me was married several times yet never had children either. She was physically abused by husbands and did not know love until later in life. Her late husband was the love of her life for almost thirty years, and he passed away after coming to know the intimate goodness of God. This sister now has a deep and passionate love relationship with God and it shows in how she cares for others. She is my next-to-oldest sister's caregiver.

My sisters and I all love the Lord, yet we each experienced an unlovely childhood from the same parents who also had unlovely childhoods.

I am the youngest daughter. I married twice and did not experience having biological children. My first husband and I should not have married, as it resulted in divorce after less than four years. We had no idea who we were and certainly had no idea how to live out life with someone else equally lost with zero direction. It is miraculous I'm even alive today. God's love rescued me. In my second and final marriage, Father God was gracious to give me two spiritual children (my husband's biological children) to love and who love me. I cannot imagine loving them more had they come from my own physical body. Over the years, we have walked out life with others who call us their spiritual parents. We are honored by their trust and love.

God showed me that the reason my siblings and I were not properly loved was because my mother and father had never been properly loved. We come from generations of men and women who were unloved and felt unlovely.

My mom's side of the family was interesting. When my grandmother (my mom's mother) was young, she was forced to marry her own father. She did divorce but the next man she married was not a nice man either.

My mother's biological brother killed himself during the Great Depression. One of my mom's sisters was locked away in a TB (Tuberculosis) asylum due to the belief it was contagious. Another sister actually drank herself to death. A third sister has a family, holds two doctorates, is a nuclear physicist and has chosen same sex attraction.

Mom had been born in what was called a poor house, and the label "poor house" was literally stamped on her birth certificate. This would be similar to a homeless shelter today but far worse, as this was after World War I and right before the Great Depression. Conditions in a poor house included unhygienic surroundings, unclean water, unhealthy environment and unsanitary bathrooms. Mom was always ashamed of her past and never allowed anyone to see her birth certificate. I saw it only after her death.

She lived next to a river with her family and did not eat beef until she was nine years old. I'm not certain if their family lived in that location due to financial issues or if it was a normal lifestyle in that day.

It is interesting to me that some of my immediate family has also experienced a homeless type of lifestyle.

My dad also came from an interesting heritage. My grandmother (dad's mother) had been married around nine times. Dad had a strong distrust for women as he experienced his mom going from man to man looking for security. His mom's generation was from the 1900's when women were not permitted to be powerful. Instead, they needed men for survival.

When my dad was a little kid, one of his jobs was to hunt for food. If he took three bullets then he was expected to bring back bullets, food or both to the family. He mentioned how he faced severe consequences for not bringing back food. He had such hurt in his eyes when sharing this information with me that I refused to ask him what kind of consequences. He could have been beaten, unfed, verbally abused or sent into isolation. Whatever it was, it was not good, and he had not recovered from the results even sixty years later.

After my mom passed, I found letters she had written but never mailed. Her writings included her begging for a friend. She expressed how lonely and unhappy she felt. In that era women were not allowed to speak about their hurts or pains. Honestly, it was a man's world. To give you an idea of how this worked, when my dad was at war, women were sent to work[1] in plants and facilities to do the jobs men could not do because of their absence. When the war was over and the "men" came home, the women were immediately dismissed and told to go home. They were expected to fulfill their jobs as homemakers. My mom's eyes glistened when she talked about working in the plant where they built airplanes. She communicated how she had appreciated earning money. Basically, what she felt when they were all fired was that they were no longer valued and their only worth was in making babies.

Now, let me share a bit about the life my parents lived together. My mom was married to my dad for thirty-six years. He was in the United States Navy for thirty years before he retired. His naval career included World War II and the Korean War. The government also called on him to participate in special projects because of his nuclear weapons expertise. When he was away, Mom experienced seasons with no food when she fed her kids from garbage cans. Are you getting the picture? It was a bleak and dreary atmosphere in her home.

I was born in 1962 and Dad came to know God in 1963, but I never knew it. My sisters were all forced to go to church and were beaten with a Bible whenever they did wrong. This was their introduction to God's love.

I'm painting a picture for you of a family who did not know unconditional love or know how to love themselves or others. They were deprived of spiritual insight, physical nutrition and emotional needs. Though you may not have experienced the same type of situation, can you relate to feeling lonely or unhappy?

This is my point: God wanted to love our family. He wanted to love my parents. It is possible someone reached out to them but perhaps he or she did not pursue relationship with my parents long enough to make an impact that would have changed our lives for the long run.

We grew up unloved and feeling unlovely.

What if Mom had cultivated a friendship with God? She would have been confident, loving, well able to maneuver into society in order to get to know others and she would have had close friends. This would have changed our entire family. What if someone had reached into Mom's life when my oldest sister had been a little girl? What if a person who knew God's love had invited her over for coffee twice a week just to chat and get to know her? What would have happened if someone had a revelation of how to love, and what if that kind of love had gotten a hold of my dad? What if someone had seen the kingdom of God as a place to love others? What would have happened to the rest of us kids had we grown up knowing God as Father, Provider, Best Friend and Closest Confidant, and not just any god to meet with on the weekend?

I believe we all would have been brought up very differently and would not have looked for love in all of the wrong places. We would have understood God's love personally. We would have had less heartbreak and pain as we grew and matured in life. We would have known how to love each other, and I believe we would have loved others better too.

I believe you will have a life-changing experience with Holy Spirit. Also, you will get to know Father and Son in a different way. Finally, you will love yourself more deeply and appreciate others even more, when you are finished with *40 Days to the BRAVE New You.*

ACKNOWLEDGEMENTS

Audra and Robert Lagoudis
You are two of the BRAVEST people I know.

Sisters Sandy and Betty
Thank you for unconditional love and support.

Bethany Martin
You are my true, steadfast, enduring friend.

Kline, Maruska & Contreras Families
Thank you for sharing your ideas with us and going through the program. We love doing life with you. Thank you for loving us.

Harlene Carter, Greg Kaufman, Ann Sontag
Thank you for reading this book. Your perspective was invaluable.

Johnette Cadis and Jennifer Greagrey
Your passion motivated me in the early days. Your encouragement was constant in the latter days.

Reverends Jill and Michael O'Brien
Honor IS what Love looks like.
You never gave up even when I did.

Pastor Bob and Sherry Phillips
Thank you for leading us into Him and showing us how to lean into one another.

Pastors Darrin and Sheila Begley

Thank you for loving our family unconditionally. Thank you for refusing to be God's voice so that I could truly become who I really am.

Pastor Lenny Weston

Thank you for seeing and giving me opportunity to be brave in your church. You encouraged me more than you will ever know. I appreciate you.

Thank you to all who reviewed the material with us over the years. You helped us find His heart.

INTRODUCTION

I struggled with fear most of my life. I know what it is like to be afraid. When I was a little girl, I would pass notes with my questions and ask my mom to write only "yes" or "no" in response. I did *not* want to hear anyone reject me. I wasn't shy. I was deathly afraid of my own shadow. Fear. It was in my face. Continually. What about you?

However, I was made to be **bold**. I was created to **respect** myself. I was created to be fearless and able to take **action** in big or small steps. Truly, I was made to be **victorious** in living and in *overcoming my past*. Finally, from very young, I was called to **encourage** myself, *and you were too*.

I did not learn how to live with this type of attitude until well into my thirties ... and then learn I did. I want to encourage you today. You are significant, you have value and you are important. Please come with Holy Spirit and me on a journey to get to know who you are. You are the most important friend you will ever have for yourself except of course, God.

BE GOOD — LOVE YOU

This is a *"be good to you, because you are awesome, and learn how to embrace yourself"* devotional and study.

This is a *"learn how to be bold, respectful, active, victorious AND encouraging for yourself"* type of devotional into more of you and more of Love.

This is a *"get to know the most powerful Partner you will ever know and the greatest Teacher whoever lived — Holy Spirit — inside you"* type of guide.

Let this season we have together encourage you to step out of any boat you are in; and maybe by the end, you will own an entire fleet of ships. This will transform the most important person in your life — *you*. You have a kingdom to explore and it all starts with you.

THIS IS ALL ABOUT YOU

This is not a typical devotional or study.

What makes this devotional different is that it is all about *you*. It is about your own identity, needs, heart, life, reality and dreams. So every week, you have five good deeds to complete for yourself. Most days, I have deeds listed for you to do for yourself. Occasionally, you get to love yourself by selecting something of your own choosing. I use the word "deed" on purpose, because this book is about *you* being intentional with you. I want to encourage and build you up. It is *not* self-help. You will be guided by Holy Spirit to be kind to the closest person you know — *you*. Train yourself to be *kind* to you.

Each day, you have the opportunity to find a way to be good to you. Why is this important? Kindness is usually learned over time — not imparted. Perhaps you love to help others and find yourself giving to people outside of you and your family all the time. But are you good to you? Do you take time for you? There is zero crime in taking time to be kind to you while living in your own home. As you consistently make room to be good to you, I believe you will see — up close — how much God loves you.

It is not how fast you accomplish a deed — it is the impact of kindness you make on yourself that matters. I give you permission to love yourself and to take action to demonstrate it. You will choose for the week what you want to do for yourself OR follow that day's suggestion. You can even check those deeds off the *Love Yourself List* as you do them. This way you keep up with your action steps — just don't allow loving yourself to turn into a *to-do list*. Let this book be the catalyst that imparts the much-needed goal of loving you and becoming a *BRAVE New You*. You may go through this study alone or ask some friends to journey with you. Just read about the small group option and go for it.

I expect you to increase your understanding in how you see, value and love yourself. Also, I expect you to gain clarity regarding how you live out your role or position in family, friendship and society. Finally, I expect you to pick up a new mantle and authority in how you impact yourself and those who live out life with you in private and public.

Journal daily and write down your thoughts, ideas, strengths and fears. I like to use an actual pen and pad but feel free to dialogue with yourself through your phone or another electronic device. You will answer questions on the daily readings.

If you decide to lead a small group, connect with me through donnareiners.com.

Let me know how you are doing. Feel free to follow me on social media. Post pictures of your journey: @donnareiners on Facebook, Instagram & Twitter.

PRAYING FOR YOU

I thank You for who You are, God. I thank You for the calling on our lives to know You more closely than we've ever known anybody. Thank You for wanting to live out life with us. Thank You for wanting us to know You intimately and personally. Thank You that You already know us and have already grabbed hold of us. Thank You for wanting our own lights to go on so we see Your life in us. How amazing that Your goodness, kindness, love, mercy and graciousness lives inside us. Father, I release strength. I release life. I pray for those struggling with emotional, mental or physical life. I release expectancy and fresh vigor into them.

I ask for boldness. Let a strong knowing of boldness rise up. Let us see who You are and what You did, so we can live in expectancy. I release a respect to resound within us for ourselves and for humanity because You live inside us.

Father, I ask for action to be taken in areas where we've been paralyzed and afraid to fail. I ask for You to show us where we shut down because we are so afraid of mistakes we might make and so afraid of criticism some people will give us when we make those mistakes. Let us move past the fear and rise up in power. Father, I ask You to show us how to be courageous and how to take action anyway. Show us how to have enough respect for ourselves to be active in areas even where people are not for us or disagree with us.

God, I ask for victory — for a victorious way of seeing life. In Your Faithfulness You arrange the heavens so we can truly see that we stand in Your victory. Because You've already won the battle, we have won the battle. As Your sons and Your daughters, we stand in the victory that has already taken place. Father, show us how to stand — how to trust again, how to believe again, how to live again ... how not to turn back but to truly take on the mantle of victory.

God, I ask for encouragement. I pray we will be encouraged. I ask when we're feeling down, defeated and shut down we will stop and take courage. I thank You that when we're going through a cycle we will stop and say, "Wait. I can recalibrate. Stop. I have courage living inside of me. Wait. I have solutions inside of me." Quicken us to realize how alive we really are as we learn to listen to the courageous One inside us.

God, I ask for Your love to manifest in us for ourselves. Father, that the love of God will become so real that we will be able to see Your love operating in our lives. In the midst of a ship breaking apart, that we can still see Your love operating in our lives because you live inside us. That we will be able to see areas where we can be thankful in the midst of things happening that are unpleasant.

God, I ask You about this whole idea of being brave. Because being brave just means to be like You. We can accomplish whatever You say. May we truly have the hope, expectancy, boldness and confidence to be brave — to be like You, instead of being pigeon-holed or living out manmade labels. We want to truly take on being a brave new us by the power of Your Holy Spirit. As we lean into our greatest Partner Who lives within us — God Almighty — we will lean into the victory that is already ours.

OPTIONAL SMALL GROUPS

If you want to lead others into bravery through this material, do not hesitate. You do not have to have any kind of *small group degree*. The only answer is listening and loving. So as a small group leader, simply study the lessons ahead of time and then go through the material with your group each week. You can read the story to the group each week and ask how everyone felt. You can easily talk through the daily devotional with your friends too.

I suggest each one of you find a friend to talk with through the week. This way, you can encourage one another. This will help you complete the book and help you process the information God gives you.

You can put your own boundaries on the time together. Prepare by praying for the participants, asking Holy Spirit to guide you, and being available to listen as your friends process the material with you. This will be a life-changing time together. Love is the only requirement. Enjoy yourself and those with you.

Allow yourself to love you more every day.

CHALLENGE 1

I AM LOVE

TEACHING — NAMELESS LOVE

In **2 Kings 5** you will find an amazing piece of history about Naaman, a highly respected army captain who had leprosy and an unnamed little girl (from the land of Israel) who waited on Naaman's wife.

2 Kings 5:1 (VOICE) "Naaman's master considered him an extraordinary man. He was the military commander of Aram's army, and he had won *many important battles* for Aram by the power of the Eternal. Naturally he was greatly esteemed by his king. Naaman was a fierce warrior, but he also had a skin disease.

2 Kings 5:2 (VOICE) ² Now *one time,* the Arameans went out in raiding parties and took a little girl from Israel as their prisoner. The little girl became a servant to Naaman's wife.

Girl *(to Naaman's wife)*: ³ If only my master could be near the prophet in Samaria, the prophet there could heal my master's disease.

2 Kings 5:4-5 (VOICE) ⁴ Naaman *became hopeful, and he* went and told his king what the little girl from Israel said.

King of Aram: ⁵ I am going to write a letter to Israel's king, and I want you to take it to him immediately."

Notice a few things:

First, some translations say Naaman was a leper. Leprosy is a contagious and detrimental skin disease, which can cause you to be deformed, without limbs and the like. Yet he was really, truly respected. He was a valiant soldier and leader. Everyone knew his name.

Second, look at the expectancy in this young servant. The little girl knew the power of the prophet and she knew the power of God.

Also, do you see what happened? The little girl who had been taken prisoner carried a message of confidence and Naaman believed. Then Naaman took action with his employer, stating out of his mouth that he could be healed. The king believed too, and he took action as well and supplied Naaman with what he needed for his journey.

2 Kings 5:5-7 ESV "So, he departed. He took with him 10 talents of silver; 6,000 shekels of gold, and 10 changes of clothing. And he brought the letter to the King of Israel, saying, 'And now, as this letter comes to you, behold: I have sent my servant Naaman to you, that you may cure his leprosy.' And it came about that when the King of Israel read the letter that he tore his clothes, and he said, 'Am I God to kill and to make alive, that this man is sending word to me to cure a man of his leprosy? But consider now and see how he is seeking a quarrel against me.'"

I find it interesting how the King of Israel immediately thought somebody was trying to set him up for a fall. Emotions kind of get in the way of Truth at times, don't they? The king was paranoid of being harmed. Yet Elisha was in tune to the king's plight.

2 Kings 5:8-13 Elisha's Message: "What has caused you to rip your clothing? Tell the man *who has come to you for healing* to come to me. Then he will be assured that a prophet lives in Israel.

⁹ *The king told Naaman to go find Elisha,* so Naaman showed up at Elisha's door with his horses and chariots. ¹⁰ Elisha *did not show his face to Naaman, but instead* sent instructions: 'Wash yourself in the Jordan River seven times. *The waters will heal you,* and your skin will be back to normal. You will be cleansed.' ¹¹ Naaman boiled with anger as he left Elisha. *He had come to his house expecting something much different.*

What is this! I came here thinking that Elisha would come outside and call upon the name of the Eternal One his God, and that Elisha's hand would pass over my sores and heal my skin disease, *not the waters of the Jordan River.* ¹² The Abanah and Pharpar Rivers in Damascus are greater rivers than all the rivers of Israel *combined,* so why couldn't I just go bathe in those and be healed?

Naaman then stormed away, boiling with anger.
¹³ Later his servants approached and spoke to him *with respect.*

Naaman's Servants: Father, if the prophet had told you to do some important thing, wouldn't you have done what he asked? Why is it difficult for you *to follow his instructions* when he tells you, 'Bathe *yourself in the Jordan River,* and be cleansed'?"

2 Kings 5:14-16 ESV So he went down and dipped himself seven times in the Jordan, according to the word of the man of God. And his flesh was restored like the flesh of a little child and he was clean. When he returned to the man of God with all his company and came and stood before him, he said, 'Behold, now I know that there is no god in all the earth but in Israel, so please take a present from your servant now.' But he said, 'As the Lord lives, before Whom I stand, I will not take anything.' And he urged him to take it, but he refused."

Word of mouth works!

The point is this little girl knew this prophet had healing power. She knew. She'd heard about him. She knew God was real. She knew God was alive. And although she had been taken captive and turned into a slave, that did not stop her from being a spokesperson for the Lord. Some people don't have the kind of relationship with their employer that gives them freedom to speak. But apparently, she felt she could. Maybe they had been kind to her? Perhaps she already had favor from God? I'm not sure but she had the guts to speak up when many people would have shut down. I find it interesting a slave girl back in that time would suggest to anyone that his or her spouse could be healed. To me it was courageous.

ATTITUDE

But Naaman chose to have a bad attitude. He was furious because the prophet didn't tell him to do some extraordinary action. Also the prophet didn't wave his hand over Naaman as if he was a magician. I pondered and I thought about the feelings and emotions he experienced. He was angry and outraged.

Did he feel entitled? Did he feel he should have been served more personally or more quickly? Think about his position as the leader of the armies and how he was accustomed to others obeying his commands. Was he inconvenienced or prideful?

Are we similar sometimes? Do we get a little impatient and just want it now? Perhaps we want more attention at times and want to personally be heard or attended to. We need recognition to feel important. In essence, could it be we have the feeling of *I want it my way and I-want-it-now way?*

I'm thanking God for the unnamed servants. All the young girl as well as the servants did was speak up. It is all they did. Then it was up to Naaman to take the necessary steps regarding his own well-being.

STUMBLING BLOCKS

Do you think at times we may suffer from feeling over responsible for the actions of others? Could this *over responsibility* be the cause of us saying "no" to obeying God or speaking up?

Maybe we think failure is inevitable so why bother? Yet is it up to us to decide for others what they will do or not do? All we can do is our part. After the little girl exercised her trust to speak up, her part was over. Next, it was up to Naaman's wife to take action to tell Naaman. In addition, it was up to Naaman to have the courage to go to his own king and say, "Hey, I heard I could be made whole." Also, it was up to the King of Aram to write a letter to the King of Israel. Everywhere there was a step of faith by each individual. Everywhere people worked together to see something happen for one person. If their steps were important, so are yours.

PERSPECTIVE

Isn't this how we're supposed to be? People who know each other, who are willing to help one another? One person doesn't have all the answers. One person may have a snippet or one small step.

Somebody else may have a greater part to play. But the one who had the smaller part is equally as important as the one who was out front and obvious. We should simply utilize our own talents and not analyze our steps to death. Sometimes we don't have a grandiose mission. We don't know what we're *about*. Sometimes we don't understand who we are because we don't have a platform to express our talent. We don't have a company where we work or we don't have a specific product we're selling. Maybe we feel insignificant and unproductive. We feel aimless as if we are not doing anything *for the Lord*. But *who* we are and *where* we are is *what* we do for the Lord. This is true whether it's cleaning your floor, washing your clothes, feeding the person with you, going to the neighbor next door or mowing somebody's lawn. Many times, what we do in our own home, family or community is more important than *grandiose* ideas.

I remember years ago in some youth groups when preachers would encourage kids to go on a mission trip. They'd teach them to go out and honor. Yet many times there was no honor at home with their parents. What if our first mission field is really at home? It seems that wherever we are, there He is, which makes our first mission field right where we're living. What if who we are and what we are doing *right here* and *right now* is as important as the going *out there*? We are unnamed women and unnamed men all over the world, and we have a mission where we live. We don't have to go to Timbuktu to tell the world about Jesus. We can tell the world about our God exactly where we are, to the people who are in our spheres of influence. To me, this is every bit as important because it is the main area God has given us to govern.

But.

But.

But.

HESITATIONS

Why do we hesitate? Fear of failure? Fear of not being heard? Fear of a negative response? Remember the little girl basically said, "Hey, the prophet can heal your husband." The wife took action but what if the wife had laughed? Or what if the prophet didn't heal him? Then the little girl would look like a fool. Isn't this how we are today? We wonder, "What if they don't get healed?" Perhaps we are afraid to look silly. We might be concerned about being validated. We may convince ourselves we have failed. Many years ago, a wise man told me that if nothing was ventured then nothing would be gained. He knew how fearful I was about living life. If we don't make our attempts or take our own steps of courage, then we really won't ever find out if X, Y or Z will ever take place.

LOVE OF GOD

Let the love of God be your compass. God's love is supposed to be what rules and reigns and lives through us. God's love to go wash the lady next door's clothes or to babysit three doors down is every bit as big as the love to go to Russia or Mexico and do mission work, or to go to the next city and bring hurricane relief.

The love of God should be the one directing us at all times, and surely He directs us right where we are already living. It is hard to believe that God would speak only if we are going to a foreign country to do good. I think we mix up momentum with the love of God.

The love of God is consistent. The love of God is faithful. The love of God is diligent. The love of God has vision and He's right here in our midst. God has been drawing me back to the simplicity of His love for me. If I love me, then that love will flow through me to others. Sometimes we want to skip over us and go to the next person, and we wonder why we're so tired and dragging. Or we wonder why we're so short-tempered. We're just going, going, going. And I don't mean giving, giving, giving — I mean going, going, going. We go, go, go, and there's no intent to our go, go, go. Perhaps we should train ourselves to stop and let God live through us. Then everyone around us will benefit. When He loves us, we have that same love to give.

TAKE ACTION

I want to encourage you to take action. If the love of God is your guide, and if there's something within you stirring, maybe it is God's idea. You won't know if you don't step out in it. You don't have to build an organization around it. Just take a few steps. See if it works. Let your thoughts be put into action. Be bold in action and be bold with loving you. Be bold with receiving love for you.

Implement your thoughts and ideas toward yourself, and you'll be bold for those around you. It is a ripple effect. You can be an influence in your corner of the world, and let the world taste the love of God in and through you.

WORDS ARE POWER

Perhaps you feel your role is not important. This is not so. It could be you feel insufficient without a visible platform to be who you want to be or say what you want to say. Just consider what happened. The young girl spoke to one woman — possibly in private — and look how it influenced an entire family. Words have power. I'm telling you leprosy is ugly stuff. I guarantee there was lack of intimacy with Naaman and his wife because of his skin disease/leprosy. Look at the restoration. He could touch again. His wife was held again. Maybe he contracted leprosy after they were married for a time. He could hug his children, if they had any.

He had the possibility of a new entrance into community with friends and family. What about the elimination of the fear of touching or being touched? I don't know. There were a lot of things restored when the leper got healed.

In addition, look how thousands of years later we are still reading of the fame of a nameless young girl. Though we do not know her name, it is with great surety I say God knows her name. She had to have an inward boldness and confidence toward herself to enable her to speak so freely. So be strong and brave, and move forward with love toward yourself and those around you.

LEPROSY OF THE HEART

Let me delineate for a moment. Maybe you've got friends or know others who have leprosy in their hearts, and they feel ugly. Inside they feel hatred for themselves. They might suffer from self-inflicted pain or harm. They don't feel like they can touch anybody, and they don't feel like they should be touched. Your word, thought or idea to love them could change their lives forever. All you can do is be faithful to love them right where they are in life. However, whether they receive this love or not is not up to you. You are only responsible to love — not responsible for the results of your love. This is why it is important you hear God and know your role to play.

You might be in a situation with someone you have loved for a long time, and that person continues to abuse you because of his or her own leprous heart. Maybe you think that same person will one day stop hurting you as long as you continue to love him or her. Perhaps you envision this individual radically changing so he or she loves you. Listen, you cannot change that person. I release you from feeling like you must put yourself in harm's way in order to heal his or her heart. I'm not convinced you being abused as you wait for the heart to change is the heart of our Father. So in the midst of me telling you to love and to trust God and to trust the process, I want you to be aware of something important. Sometimes the process of loving someone takes place after you are long gone from your part in that process. Love takes time and it does work but sometimes love works later.

BEHIND THE SCENES

Let's return to my original intention, which is for you to understand your own importance and purpose. Your love is meaningful and what you do behind the scenes is powerful. Take on this truth — it is good that we remain nameless and faceless at times. We can be faithful with God living through us and we can change our part of the world — one person at a time.

LOVE YOURSELF LIST

Pace yourself. REVIEW AND CHOOSE for the week what you want to do for yourself OR follow each day's suggestion. Check them off as you do them. You can use these ideas any time you want.

- Bake or buy a special dessert/treat.
- Make plans to go to the movies.
- Organize or clean a closet, your kitchen or other area of your house, apartment or room.
- Send yourself an electronic card, and schedule it to be delivered the following week.
- Take time to be kind to you.
- Smile at yourself in the mirror five times today.
- Hug yourself three times today.
- Write, "Have a Good Day!" on your mirror.
- Write a note that says, "Have a Great Day!" and leave it on your desk, refrigerator or in your car.
- Write yourself an encouraging letter and snail mail to yourself.
- Email yourself your favorite phrase.
- Hold your own hand for at least one minute. Think about how a good friend will not let go of you and how you are a good friend for you. While you hold your hand, say to yourself, "I will not let go of me."
- Take yourself out for coffee. Enjoy yourself. Do not be afraid of the silence and enjoy you.

- Write down what is good about you.
- Write down some of your ideas.

DAY 1. WHAT IS LOVE?

Love is so interesting. Love is an action word in God's economy. He is Love. When I read this verse, I read it as God does not act unbecomingly, and He seeks what is best for us. He is not provoked, and He does not take into account wrongs. He loves us, and this is why we can forgive ourselves and others.

My Mind — **1 Corinthians 13:5 NASB** Love does not act unbecomingly; it does not seek its own, is not provoked, it does not take into account a wrong suffered.

My Mouth — I am forgiving and I am kind toward myself. I refuse to hold my own mistakes or errors against me.

My Move — *OK, so this will seem strange but just do it.* Today I am holding my own hand for at least 60 seconds. I will think about how a good friend will not let go of me and how I am a good friend for myself. I will not give up on me.

Reflection Time

Ask yourself: Do I give up on me? How can I stop giving up?

What did I discover about myself today?

Did I feel awkward holding my own hand? Did it feel strange to think of anyone holding me and not wanting to let me go?

How can I not give up on me? What steps can I take to improve my own personal tenacity?

Spend 10 minutes in praise & 10 minutes in prayer.

Consider this: Think about how God will not let you go. He is a good friend. He will not let you go. Even if you let Him go — He does not let you go. He will not allow you to go away from Him. God is holding you. He refuses to forsake you. He is for you and not against you. He lives inside you, and He wants you to love you.

DAY 2. I AM AT PEACE

There is a perfect peace we can have when we keep our minds on God and trust Him with our lives. Peace is a tremendous reflection of His love. Does it make sense to you that if we think of Him (Love) then we can be at peace?

My Mind — I am at peace within myself and with others. What does peace look like to me?

My Mouth — I choose to trust You all the days of my life. I gladly think of You and Your love for me. I'm so grateful Your Son died for me so I can live in You and with You.

My Move — I will sit and visualize a river flowing deep in me and beside me. Can I see it?

Reflection Time

How do I remain at peace with myself and others?

What was my action today in the area of peace?

How do I define peace? **Ephesians 6:15** talks about the Gospel of Peace and that word peace[2] in this instance means 'to join peace, prosperity, rest and quietness.' Does this peace live in me? Do I gladly seek God's face? How?

Spend 10 minutes in praise & 10 minutes in prayer.

Optional Reading — Isaiah 26:3 NLT You will keep in perfect peace all who trust in You, all whose thoughts are fixed on You!

Consider this: Situations arise with an agenda to pull you off course and chop you into little pieces. You have the opportunity to choose not to be shaken. You get to choose to remain in peace instead of pieces. You can choose to trust the God of Peace. It truly is a choice. I have had to make this decision. It was deep inside me. It was a thought. An idea. A feeling. I had to remember His love in the challenge. I had to remember He died for me too. It became a game changer to remain in peace when my circumstances screamed chaos. You and I can both choose a better pathway. Because of the Love of God inside of you and inside of me, when we are facing trouble or conflict, we can stay calm. Choose with me to give Him all your brokenness. Choose with me to give Him everything inside you that feels split apart. Remain in peace. Remain in rest.

DAY 3. CHRIST'S CONNECTION

What a calling we have to imitate God as beloved children. How do we imitate someone we cannot see? God is Love. Loving Him and others is one way we demonstrate Him to the world. Trusting Him like a little child is another way. Trust Love as if you were jumping into the arms of someone you trust in the water, and imagine Him catching and holding you in the deep.

My Mind — I am made in God's image, and Christ lives inside me. That means I can love myself right here and right now.

My Mouth — I follow Christ's example and imitate my Father God. I esteem myself and delight in myself just as I delight in others. I am as a child, and I trust You and those You have sent to love me.

My Move — I'm choosing now to delight in myself. I am taking myself out to dinner or coffee. I will spend time delighting in Him and I will let Him delight in me. My intention is to spend time with myself and to listen to Holy Spirit — to go on a date out and see what He reveals to me.

Reflection Time

How do I walk in love?

Did I take myself out to dinner or coffee?

Did I practice delighting in my own company?

Do I feel myself becoming increasingly BRAVE in how I view myself?

Spend 10 minutes in praise & 10 minutes in prayer.

Optional Reading — Ephesians 5:2 NLT Live a life filled with love, following the example of Christ. He loved us and offered himself as a sacrifice for us, a pleasing aroma to God.

Consider this: You are not horrible and you are not worthless, no matter what you have done. You have value, and God is all in. He is for you. Connect with Him. You have significance. Esteem yourself. Delight in yourself as you delight in others. Trust God, my friend. Love yourself in a different way today. Spend time with Him and yourself. Intentionally spend time with you instead of running around. Stop. Don't run from you today. Stop. Spend time with you today. Let Him show you that you are His favorite. You are His beloved. He loves you. You can love you too.

DAY 4. LOVE LOOKS IN ON ME

How do God's commandments show He loves me? The New Covenant is not about obeying the perfection of the rules but rather showing we love Him. Honestly, we get to obey God from the perspective of relationship. He does not ask of us anything we are incapable of completing.

My Mind — **1 John 5:3 ESV** For this is the love of God: that we keep His commandments and His commandments are not burdensome.

My Mouth — God's commandments are not a heavy burden for me. I am well able to yield to both the simplest and the most complicated idea from God because He lives inside me. His love for me is so great that I can't help but be drawn into His benevolence and good intentions for me. I want to show Him my love.

My Move — Today I want to just lie still in quiet and consider this amazing love God has for me … so great that the Father gave His own Son for me. What a great and incredible love. I'm not going to *do* anything other than be still. I am going to find a place where I can listen quietly to my own heart beating. I'm going to listen to my own thoughts and hear His thoughts of love for me.

If nothing comes to mind in my quiet time, then I consider these words: Love looks in on me. Love is pursuing me. Love is looking back at me in the mirror with a smile of contentment. If I am Love, then I can be loved.

Reflection Time

Do I believe Love looks in on me? This is personal. God lives within me. Another word for God is Love. I am making a transition from thinking God is only a spiritual being. I am choosing to trust He is Love. I'm choosing to trust this Love flows from Him to me. Also, I'm choosing to trust Love flows through me to others.

How did I experience God's love?

Can I commit to having more moments thinking about His love for me?

Spend 10 minutes in praise & 10 minutes in prayer.

Optional Reading — 1 John 5:4 ESV For everyone who has been born of God overcomes the world. And this is the victory that has overcome the world — our faith.

Consider this: I hope you know you are not alone and not forsaken. God is for you. I love you. Has anyone said, "I love you" lately? I want you to hear it from me. I love you. God loves you. Let's talk about New Covenant Love. God is not angry with you. He is not mad at you. His intentions for you are good, kind, compassionate, loving and gracious. He is not thinking evil about you. He is not thinking about the bad you have done or how He needs to correct or straighten you out. And if for some reason He highlights something that He wants you to change, it is from a motive of love.

DAY 5. I NEED OTHERS

A transaction took place when Jesus died on the cross. He trusted the Father. He embraced us. He never needed us but we do need Him. And because He calls us to be in community, we need one another too. We learn from one another. We receive love from one another. We receive restoration through community. We can love one another too.

My Mind — I need others. Do I enjoy others?

My Mouth — I belong to God. He is my Father. I am the builder of His family name. I need God. I belong to the One Who created the entire universe. What a Partner for my lifetime. Father God's church is my family, and I need others who are in close relationship with Him to speak into my life.

My Move — I am going to look myself in the eye and tell myself I am thankful for my own friendship. I'm going to take time to encourage myself on this journey to discover a *braver* me. I will make an appointment on my calendar to go shopping, hunting, fishing or sightseeing with Holy Spirit. I may go play golf or go to lunch or go to the movies. I thank God He is my Companion and I'll share with Him how I'm walking out this season of intimacy.

Reflection Time

What do I believe about trusting God in my personal life? Do I expect Him to be good? Am I confident of His love?

Do you ever consult others for their ideas, or do you work more as a lone ranger — autonomously? Be honest. There is no sin in honesty. How can you *not* be a lone ranger? Do you feel God is your Partner in life or that He is up in the sky and untouchable?

Spend 10 minutes in praise & 10 minutes in prayer.

Optional Reading — John 14 in any translation

Consider this: Look at yourself and be thankful for you. Sometimes our lives can *feel* lonely. Sometimes friends are nowhere to be found. Believe in you anyway. Be there for you anyway. Even though people betray you, it doesn't mean God does not love you. Don't face joy alone without God. Don't face trouble alone without God. Perhaps Jesus was lonely at times also. We know Jesus was often misunderstood and left hanging by His apostles. Yet He persevered. He did not turn back. He did not give in to those thoughts. He knew Father was for Him. He kept moving toward His purpose, and you can too.

LOVE TAKEAWAY

You are completely loved.

God is bigger than you think.

He is not judging you.

He is not telling you to get yourself together.

He is well able to put you together.

He loves you right where you are in Him.

Before going into the next section, please consider how you are truly, completely loved without any conditions placed on you to be perfect in your heart or actions.

CHALLENGE 2

I AM BOLD

TEACHING — ARE YOU BOLD?

The book of **Acts** is fascinating. These are stories, problems, actions and life-changing moments in history, all in the name of Jesus. These writings are significant because they tell how the early Church was formed through the actions of the Apostles. The setting is tribulation and persecution.

Jesus had come on the scene and left a group of men and women behind to carry on His message of the Good News. They took the mandate very seriously. They had witnessed the actions of Jesus. They knew He was the real deal. Some had seen Him die and resurrect, and they knew He was good for what He had said. His promise not to leave them alone was true, and it made them bold and strong.

Read **Acts 27,** the entire chapter, in any translation. Lean into Paul's strength, and learn how he handled an impossible and seemingly hopeless situation.

SHIPWRECK

One of the strongest stories from our history in the book of **Acts** is when Paul was in a storm, and he commanded all of the people to remain in the boat when they wanted to jump out. An angel visited Paul and assured him they would live and fulfill their assignment. He heard from God and was able to share what he heard with those on the ship, causing all of them to expect better of their circumstances. Expectancy rose up in them to believe they would live and not die.

I've been seriously thinking about how we need to live *bold*. God lives inside us. I know sometimes we don't feel like we are bold. Sometimes we have absolutely crazy situations. We wonder what the heck we're going to do, how the heck we're going to get out of whatever is going on and how we will find a solution.

Let's begin a new kind of self-talk. Let's be expectant of God's goodness. Let's choose to believe it's going to be good regardless of what we go through. He's in you. He's got purpose. Where the enemy comes to kill, steal and destroy, God has come to bring you a life that has His abundance. It may not feel like your life is going to be abundant. It may not feel like life is very good. It might look like all hell has broken loose in you, around you and in front of you. However, it does not mean you can't move forward into the storm. We have storms to face. What if we switch perspective? What if when we are exhausted and about to give up, we decide to switch into fifth gear? Let's become the storm. That's right. Let's decide we won't be overcome, but we will be the ones doing the overcoming. We need to be a storm of boldness. We need to know that we know that we know that it's going to be all right. Somehow we've got to decide it's going to be more than good. Before the storm rolls in, we need to decide we have already overcome.

DON'T BE THE MARTYR

Look at what happened in **Acts 26**, when the Apostle Paul was confronted with people who wanted to stop him. They wanted to destroy him, kick his booty and get him out of there. What happened? He appealed to Caesar, which was his ticket to stay alive. Sometimes we think, "Just be the martyr." No, don't be the martyr. God wants you to live. God wanted Paul to live. God didn't want his life to end right then. God wants you to live. Why? First, He loves you. Second, He's your Father. Third, there's a purpose and a plan moving through you right this moment. You don't want to abort the process of what God wants to do in and through you.

GOD IS AT WORK

Now, what if you feel stagnant? Just because it doesn't feel like God is doing anything in or through you doesn't mean He isn't. Sometimes we feel as though God is silent. Because we have the perspective there is nothing significant going on in our lives, we figure there's no way anything important is happening. Maybe that's when God is doing the deepest work in us and doing things around us we don't even know. We're not even cognizant that we are growing. We don't see our own changes because we are entrenched in the middle of it all and blinded by the challenges. Sometimes we get lost in our own storms, problems and situations. We become self-conscious and think our lives are out of control. We don't realize we are still demonstrating to the world that God is good. God is faithful. God is kind. God loves. God is compassionate. God is merciful. God has a plan.

In **Acts 26, 27 and 28** you can see the mercy of God working with Paul. It says even the great Paul lost all hope — all expectancy. Then God sent an angel to strengthen him and tell him, "It's going to be OK. You're going to live. Everybody is going to live. Just do what I tell you to do." Sometimes we just need to obey the Lord and do what He tells us to do. Do it even if you feel afraid.

YOU HAVE COME TOO FAR

Recently, I was talking with somebody who was overrun with thought patterns reminding her of her past failures. As those thoughts continued, she felt as if she was not going to make it and her future was going to be just like her past. Those are all lies. She's gone too far to go back now. You've gone too far to go back now. Don't go back. Move forward. Don't retreat. Look ahead of you. This is what Paul did. He warned them. He said, "Look, if you don't do what I tell you, it's not going to go down right." At one point in time, the guards wanted to kill all of the prisoners on board the ship. Paul had a different worldview in place and he refuted the guard's intention to destroy them. In order to better understand, read where Paul told his story about meeting Jesus, and how they then took him on a ship (because he appealed to Caesar).

YOU WILL MAKE IT TO SHORE

Then the ship completely broke apart, and he made it to shore with nothing but a piece of wood. It was only a plank from the boat but he made it to shore. And when Paul arrived, all sorts of happenings took place for the glory of God. I guarantee it didn't feel like the glory of God. I guarantee he didn't feel glorious when he felt as if he was going to die.

Paul was a human being like you and me. He lived by the Spirit of God the way you and I live by the Spirit of God. At any given moment, he could have chosen to give up. At any given moment, he could have chosen to jump off the ship and say, "I'm done with this." But he didn't.

DON'T JUMP SHIP

Don't jump off the ship. What I mean is don't leave Him. Don't leave the only One who can walk with you through it — God Himself. If you're going to do any kind of retreating, *retreat into Christ*. Decide now to yield to Christ. Yield to His thoughts and ideas that always point to life. Your mind may be saying, "I'm a failure. I'm not going to make it. I just need to give up and kill myself. I have lived long enough. I'm won't survive this time. I am trapped. Things are never going to change."

Listen, any thought that leads you away from living is not from Him. Is it a literal spirit speaking? I don't know. Could it be just emotions or patterns of *stinkin' thinkin'* from the past? Is your past attempting to convince you that you're never going to move into anything different? Lies. Do not believe those thoughts. Do not trust *those* ideas.

NOW IS YOUR PURPOSE

I want to encourage you today to gird up some fresh strength, make a different decision, have a new thought, stop and recalibrate. Where are you going? Are you flowing in defeat? Are you growing in self-pity? Are your thoughts, "Woe is me. This is horrible. I hate my life. Oh, how I dread tomorrow!" If those are your thoughts, I want you to stop. I want to help you recalibrate your mind. Will you do an exercise with me? I want you to bring all the yucky thoughts into your focus and I want you to see those thoughts in your own hands. I want you to picture your hands throwing them down a garbage disposal. Visualize the water running. Listen to those thoughts being chopped into little unrecognizable pieces and bits. Imagine it ground up into mush and then watch it wash down the pipe never to return back up again.

Say this with me: "Wait. I'm alive on purpose. I may not know what the vision is but I'm alive for a reason, or I would not still be breathing." The very breath you have belongs to God Almighty. You were made in His image. You are breathing. There is purpose for you. I'm also telling you: When this life is up, there's purpose for you then too. But right now, our purpose is now. Your purpose is now. It is not next week, not a year from now and not 10 years from now. Your purpose is now.

RECALIBRATE

So stop, recalibrate and rethink your *unkind thoughts* and give yourself a break. Have mercy over yourself. Be patient with yourself. Be kind to yourself. Quit giving in to the voices, thoughts and ideas that want to take you into utter darkness and despair. Maybe rejection was your best friend 10 years ago, and it's circled back around to see if you'll come into agreement with it? Is it possible those negative agreements want to be close and chummy again? Or maybe depression, sadness or grief is knocking on the doorway to your mind. Let's take this a step further. Could it be you were offended with something years ago, and all of a sudden you find the same emotion of offense rising up in you? Listen: If you don't deal with it, it's going to remain your companion. All of these emotions want to remind you of your past self — but you do not have to let it happen. Are you willing to say goodbye to turmoil?

I bless you today. You know, I'm an emotions coach. I love to help people work through their feelings. And let me tell you something. I understand these emotions because my feelings rise up to control me, and I have to deal with them. We must refuse to be overwhelmed and overtaken by emotions. I'm not giving you anything I don't have to give myself. I can't always meet with every single one of you due to limited time or booked schedules, but I can pray for you.

PRAYING FOR YOU

Father, I pray for people who are being overwhelmed with their emotions. Their feelings want them to sink their own ship. In the name of Jesus, we cancel this assignment off their life now, and we release them from pieces into peace. We gather up all of the pieces, and we put all of those pieces in Your hands, Jesus. We release the peace of God that surpasses all understanding. I'm asking You to bring a new thought pattern into their minds. Give them a new opportunity to think differently. Give them a new chance to have a thought filled not with despair but with joy. Give them a new time to yield to the One who is their very strength. Realign them with Your mind. Realign them with Your thoughts. Realign them with Your love.

SPEAKING TO YOU

Realign. I release realignment into your spirit, soul and body so you will see God is for you.

I want you to say with me, "I'm for me." I want you to decide right now you're for yourself. "God is for me, and I am for me. Though that person over there might not be for me, I'm choosing to be for me this day, because it's my new day."

I bless you today. I pray you will know God loves you. He wants something different for you. He wants something good for you — something from Him. I pray you will recognize it when it comes along, and you will not be distracted by emotions that want to prevent you from seeing it. Because of Jesus, I bless you today.

I encourage you to read **Acts 26, 27 and 28**. Look what happened with Paul. Look how he handled those situations. And just know you can trust to look back one day and see how you overcame.

LOVE YOURSELF LIST

You have five good deeds to accomplish for yourself. Though you might be tempted to do all five deeds in one day, I suggest you spread them out so you can train yourself to be kind to you. Kindness is learned — not imparted. Remember, it is not how fast you accomplish a kind deed. It is the impact you make on yourself from that action of love or kindness.

Review this list and choose your deeds for the week, or choose a suggestion daily. Note I asked you to compliment yourself a lot. Why? Because habits are hard to break and start ... So intentionally begin to tell your subconscious that you are for you.

- Compliment yourself on your clothes 10 times.
- Compliment yourself on your hair 10 times.
- Compliment yourself on a specific ability 10 times.
- Smile at yourself in the mirror 10 times.
- Compliment your character and personality.
- Tell yourself aloud how much you appreciate you. Look into your eyes in the mirror and speak with sincerity.
- Buy yourself a meaningful card and write yourself a note in it; then mail it to yourself via the U.S. Post Office.
- Dress really nice — like you are worth a million bucks — and then take yourself to dinner. You don't have to go someplace expensive — you can go wherever you want.

DAY 6. PETER

Peter was something else. He was strong-willed, strong-minded, and by all appearance a bit rambunctious. Yet Jesus loved him so much that He told him He was going to build His church with him. Peter started out as a fear-filled man who did not want others to know he was associated with Jesus. Peter became a right-hand man who accomplished mighty acts by the power of Christ. Holy Spirit even visited him regarding food that was considered taboo for his culture. Christ told Peter to change his mind about what he felt was unclean according to Jewish tradition. In **Acts 10:9-23**, Jesus led Peter to change his mind about his traditions and to embrace the cleanness that came only through the grace of God.

My Mind — I am strong and able to carry the mantle Jesus has for me. I am making a change of mind in personal areas of defeat.

My Mouth — I will not turn back. I will press forward into change. I know my change is connected to my future. I will be a doorway of destiny for others.

My Move — I am looking at my life and making fresh decisions regarding my past. If I have been in denial in any way, I am girding myself up for the next part of the journey to follow Jesus into my destiny. I have purpose. I will be successful. I take dominion where I have not conquered before. I am making a list now of three areas I can change. I am choosing to be bold and unafraid as I press forward into embracing more of God and more of me. I am choosing to see my future as possible.

Reflection Time

What are three measurable and doable things I can accomplish in a short amount of time to encourage myself as I move forward?

What are the steps I took? Did I complete them?

Spend 10 minutes in praise & 10 minutes in prayer.

Optional Reading — **Matthew 26:69-75** This will tell you how Peter denied Christ, as Jesus said he would do. Find any translation and read these few verses for yourself.

Consider this: Peter had to embrace a change of mind about how he saw himself after he denied Christ. Forgiveness could be found only through the grace of God. I encourage you to embrace a change of mind about yourself. I want you to consider truly being bold about yourself and the life you live instead of hiding behind any of your own self-made rules of protection. You might even be hiding behind rules someone else made for you many years ago. Today is the day to let it go. You are strong. You are able to hold the mantle Jesus has for you. I encourage you to find an area in which you feel disappointed or discouraged, and make a plan. Figure out a way to follow up and follow through, so you can face defeat and put it behind you in that specific area of your life. Concentrate on that area for at least a week or so. You may need a month or even a few months. You will know when you have overcome.

DAY 7. KILLER TO LOVER

In Acts 9:1-19, we enter into a story about a man named Saul who was born again on the road to Damascus. The Father blinded him through light and revealed His Son inside him. Saul, now turned Paul, began a personal journey with Holy Spirit. He had been a bold, law-driven Pharisee. Enter: Jesus Himself. Can you imagine what it must have been like to hear the voice of Father God? Think of the paradigm change he made. He was a Pharisee of Pharisees and killed Christians. He persecuted those who followed Christ. He disappeared fourteen years one time. He disappeared for a period of three years another time. He even submitted what the Lord showed him to those who led the church. He boldly approached those he once hated. Paul had probably killed some of their friends, sisters, brothers, fathers or mothers. He boldly made himself accountable to the apostles who were in place. He spent years killing those he hated just to give himself over to a lifestyle that caused others to want to kill him. Saul, a radical killer, experienced a name change to Paul, a radical lover of Christ — from a radical sold out Pharisee to a radical sold out Apostle.

My Mind — I am accountable and willing to make radical changes in how I think and how I view life. I want to know God.

My Mouth — I'm a conqueror and live by His faith.

My Move — Today I'm conducting a personal inventory to consider how I think and how I look at life. Is there a specific area I need to look more like Christ?

Reflection Time

What do I think about Paul and his willingness to submit himself to the ones he used to hate? Have I ever had to approach people I used to mistreat?

Spend 10 minutes in praise & 10 minutes in prayer.

Optional Reading — Galatians 1:11 – 2:2 (any translation)

Consider this: God's faith lives literally within us. This is not just a little faith. **Colossians** says the Godhead lives inside of us. Father, Son, and Holy Spirit live inside you and live inside me. Therefore, we have more than just a little bitty measure of trust. We have the trust of Jesus Christ the Son of God living inside of us. We can do whatever He wants us to do and become whoever He wants us to become. We can live the life of passion, dedication, purpose and joy He's called us to.

DAY 8. GIRL TO MOTHER

The angel Gabriel appeared before Mary. His message was clear. She was to carry the Son of God in her womb. She had much to ponder and consider. Could it be the supernatural was not foreign to her? Look at the way she responded to the angel. What a game changer for life. Yes, she had planned to marry, but it was not her plan to marry already pregnant. Can you imagine knowing you were carrying the One who would die for your sins? After having the Child, she and Joseph were on the run for a season as the Father sought to protect the Son from being murdered. Carrying the Son of God was not a happy-go-lucky assignment. It was serious business and required angelic protection, divine inspiration and creative ideas to survive.

My Mind — I am determined not to lean into my own understanding but to listen and lean into God.

My Mouth — I trust the process God has me in to hear from Him and to pursue His purposes.

My Move — I have a divine assignment that requires more of me than ever before, so I am determined to get in prayer, get into praise and trust Him with my process.

Reflection Time

Mary and Joseph both went along with the angel and obeyed and trusted God with their lives.

What a responsibility!

How do I think I would have handled such an assignment?

Spend 10 minutes in praise & 10 minutes in prayer.

Optional Reading — Matthew 1-2; Luke 1-2 any translation: the story of Mary and Joseph

Consider this: Have you had an assignment from Christ that was not your norm? Did it take you far beyond your comfortable boundaries? Have you ever had to rely heavily on the supernatural for protection and direction as God called you forward? Being a Christian is not for wimps. It could not have been easy for Mary to be told she would become pregnant. Yet, remember how she responded? She said, "Let it be unto me, my Lord, unto Your will." Do you do that when you get an assignment from God? Do you say, "Whatever You want, God?"

DAY 9. SICK TO WHOLE

In **Luke 8:43-48 (VOICE),** the story of the woman with the issue of blood is profound.

[43] In the crowd was a woman. She had suffered from an incurable menstrual disorder for 12 years [and had spent her livelihood on doctors with no effect].[b] *It had kept her miserable and ritually unclean, unable to participate fully in Jewish life.* [44] *She followed Jesus,* until she could reach Him. She touched the fringe of the robe Jesus wore, and at that moment the bleeding stopped.

Jesus *(stopping and looking about)*: [45] Who touched Me?

Some in the Crowd *(everyone speaking at once)*: Not me.

Another in the Crowd: It wasn't me either.

Peter [and those with him][c] *(intervening)*: Master, what kind of question is that, with this huge crowd all around You and many people touching You on all sides?

Jesus: [46] *I felt something.* I felt power going out from Me. I know that somebody touched Me.

[47] The woman now realized her secret was going to come out sooner or later, so she stepped out of the crowd, shaking with fear, and she fell down in front of Jesus. Then she told her story in front of

everyone—why she touched Him, what happened as a result.

Jesus: [48] Your faith has made you well again, daughter. Go in peace.

This woman had literally exhausted all her resources to be healed. She was desperate. She was probably out of money and out of time. Perhaps she was anemic after so many years of struggle, and maybe she was close to death. We don't know the entire story, but we do know enough. She had heard of this Jesus who restored the health of others and she secretly reached for the hem of His robe expecting to be healed. The Lord said her faith made her whole. Interesting as I chew on what this meant for her future. In that day, she was considered unclean through Jewish Law. Jewish Law demanded someone announce his or her uncleanliness when around others. After she was healed, she no longer had to yell her past ailment to the world. Why? Because she was unclean no more. She could be a normal person. Wow. I don't even know what I would do. Do you? Gratitude had to have grabbed her attention. It would have mine. She would have to be bold in living life as clean forever forward. It's possible she had no friends, little to no family and no community due to her illness. She would now have to boldly make new changes in how she approached life and living, friendships and community …
Other people would have to change too. In other

words, she became the change. She was changed, so everyone around her would have to change too. Wow!

My Mind — I am a new person because God lives inside me. I want God to show me how to move forward in my newness.

My Mouth — I am pressing into the newness of who I am *becoming* through His Spirit inside me.

My Move — I'm going to take authority over me. I'm making changes in how I approach myself and how I invite God into my private world.

<u>Reflection Time</u>

Have I ever made such a radical change that it demanded I treat myself differently and others treat me differently too? What happened?

Spend 10 minutes in praise & 10 minutes in prayer.

Optional Reading — **Matthew 9:20; Mark 5:25**

Consider this: Who does God say you are? Who do you say you are? A time comes in all our lives when we need to have an attitude adjustment regarding how we treat ourselves. It could be you are not treated with much worth. Could it be that you do not treat yourself with worth either?
I suggest you begin to speak to yourself with a higher regard, and in time others will as well.

DAY 10. ADAM TO JESUS

Our assignments change from time to time, but our true purpose does not. From early on, humanity was told to dominate the world. Adam was assigned the task of replenishing the earth, naming the animals, multiplying and working the ground. It was all part of a strategy to take charge and carry responsibility. Fast forward to now. See Jesus Who has declared, "It is finished." His assignment to die and be resurrected is complete. His purpose to provide eternity for us is still being worked through as He intercedes for us twenty-four hours a day, seven days a week. Sometimes we pray for years about taking action in an area, and by the time we think we have a *yes* in the area of inquiry, the window has passed. Then we need to wait for another window. We get to abide in Christ and spend time with our Father. This is where we get to know His heart and mind for our lives and what He wants us to do. But if we are continually with Him, won't He show us as we go along? Our purpose is to carry Him wherever we go — to seize opportunities He gives us and tell others about Christ. We are still to replenish the earth with His will and multiply on planet earth those who follow Him. Within whatever job we are assigned we are to dominate, excel and own it. We are to increase His Spirit with His gifts and light and to bear fruit. We must be bold as we move forward.

My Mind — I am bold and able to complete my assignment.

My Mouth — God did not create me to live in fear. I am bold with the mind of Christ.

My Move — This is my new day. I'm stopping to determine my purpose and understand what my assignments are within that purpose.

Reflection Time

Do I have a purpose? Do I know my current assignment? If so, how am I going to accomplish it? I may have no idea where to begin, so I'm going to begin with simply writing down my thoughts. I acknowledge You and listen for Your voice, Father.

Spend 10 minutes in praise & 10 minutes in prayer.

Optional Reading — Hebrews 7:25 ESV
Consequently, He is able to save to the uttermost those who draw near to God through Him since He always lives to make intercession for them.

Romans 8:26-27 NLT And the Holy Spirit helps us in our weakness. For example, we don't know what God wants us to pray for. But the Holy Spirit prays for us with groanings that cannot be expressed in words. And the Father Who knows all hearts knows what the Spirit is saying, for the Spirit pleads for us believers in harmony with God's own will.

Consider this: We have to know God's heart and mind. We have to know He is for us, and our purpose is simple. It's to take over the world with His love and message that says His mercy triumphed over judgment at the cross. This sounds so grandiose, doesn't it? What I mean is to take over the part of your world where you live. Wherever you are, there He is. Wherever you are, it is up to you to take charge, encourage, strengthen, love and stay unified with Him. It is important that your belief of Him living inside of you remain strong. That means wherever you are is your sweet spot. Don't relinquish your spot, but take charge of it and start with you. Start inside your own mind, heart and emotions. Start with loving you, being kind to you and seeing the good inside of you. Take those chances that might be opportunities to see and experience His love. One friend asked me if this takeover is about reaching our highest potential in God. Our greatest and highest potential is found only in knowing Christ. As you lean into Him, He leads you into how to live your life with confidence and fullness right where you spend your every day.

BOLD TAKEAWAY

Look at your life and make fresh decisions.

If you have been in denial in any way, gird yourself up for the next part of your journey to follow Jesus instead of denial.

You have purpose. You are successful.

Take dominion where you have not conquered before.

Today's a new day. Don't turn back. Don't give in to those voices that want you to live in defeat. Press into more of God, more of you and more of your purpose.

Before going into the next section on respect, I want you to choose three measurable and doable things you can do in a short amount of time to encourage yourself. Complete them before moving forward.

1.

2.

3.

Be bold, my friend. You have value. You are worth it. Go for it! This will chip away at the emotions of defeat and help them stay in your past instead of your present.

CHALLENGE 3

I AM RESPECT

TEACHING — RESPECT YOU?

Have you ever heard the song, "R-E-S-P-E-C-T"? This song[3] was written in 1965 by Otis Redding and the lyrics reinforced the traditional role of a woman who was supposed to respect her husband's provision for the home. However, it was rebirthed and made famous by Aretha Franklin in 1967 with a twist for men to earn the respect of women. It was a powerful statement in the sixties that brought a new power to feminism.

I've been thinking about the word *respect*. What does respect mean? We talk about respecting ourselves. But some time back, someone asked me if I thought God respected us. I thought, "What an idea." Honestly, I pondered it a while because I had never really considered it. But the more I mulled it over, the more the answer was, "Yes. He does respect us." He respects us enough to give us free will. He gave us the freedom to choose. We can choose Him or not choose Him. The freedom to choose is a sign of respect.

You know, many of us raise our kids with no choices. Why? Because we're afraid they're going to make a mistake and screw something up. We don't want them to make the mistakes we made. I get it. But the freedom to choose is important.

WE HAVE FREEDOM

God gives us the freedom to make up our own minds. See, this is the thing. As people, we need to give guidance to our kids. God gives us guidance. He's a good Father. He's a *good* Father, and He wants to guide and lead us. But at the end of the day, He is going to allow us either to align with Him or not align with Him. He gave us the freedom to choose. Why? Because God is not a control freak. Many of us have control issues, but God doesn't have those. Father God freely sent His Son Jesus, and Jesus freely said *yes*. There wasn't a control thing in there. This was a covenant They made with One Another. A covenant is freely given. It's freely received. It is an exchanged life. Father and Son made this unbreakable covenant with One Another on behalf of humanity, and then Jesus died on a cross for our sins and our healing. They did this without our help or our *yes*. However, we get to choose to receive the benefits of Their decision.

FORGIVENESS ON HIS LIPS

In **Acts Chapter 7** we pick up the life of Stephen, and we witness a history lesson spoken aloud to what was known as the Council. At this point, he has been falsely accused and stands before both his accusers and those who are charged with judging him as guilty or innocent. Stephen speaks for almost all of Chapter 7, where he makes his case strongly and succinctly, with confidence and power. He so angers those before him that they stone him to death. What a way to die! His last words resonate throughout history, "Lord, do not hold this sin against them!" Stephen was stoned to death, and he died with forgiveness on his lips. What courage.

TRUTH GIVER

Perhaps you are wondering how this meshes with respect. Well, the thought is Stephen could have lied. He could have made something up to get free from the predicament. He could have been afraid of what would happen if he told the absolute truth. But he told the truth. He did not defend himself. He not defend Jesus. But he talked about Jesus. Stephen spoke about who God was, what God did and what it meant for everyone. To me that is very, very powerful. His testimony was about the report of the Lord. It wasn't even about himself. And he was killed for it. Stephen knew to Whom he belonged. He knew he had freedom to speak his mind about Who this real God was inside him and what the reality of what God was for them. He had deep insight into their calloused hearts. Why? Because he had a personal relationship with God. His relationship was so personal that He had no fear speaking the truth to people who hated his message. This is not about religion. All his audience understood was religion. The ones who killed Stephen only understood the Law. They knew only Old Covenant, which was only religion. This was Stephen's moment. We all have a day that comes … the time in all of our lives when we must grab hold of The One Who has us and truly decide He is real, His life within us is real, and it is time to actually live *real life*. Stephen knew who (and Whose) he was. He had lived life already performing signs, wonders and miracles, and he knew deep inside that his life was not his own.

RELATIONSHIP OF RESPECT

It was being obedient. Obedient. Obedient … We get to be obedient now as well, of course. But we do it out of relationship, not because we're going to be afraid of this or that happening to us or around us. It is about relationship with a real Person Who offers us life on this planet and after we leave this planet. Perhaps our freedom to choose *is* God's respect for us. And He sent us the Holy Spirit so we can have Him as a Person help us make decisions. But you know what? At the end of the day, we can still choose to rebel. We can still choose to say no. He gave us the freedom to choose. Inside my mind and heart, I see that as the greatest place of respect. We too give respect when we give others freedom to choose.

God is not trying to beat you up. God as a Father is not slapping you upside the head and saying, "I'm mad at you. I'm disturbed at you. You did the wrong thing." Whap. Whap. Whap. You know, we had parents who did that mess to us. But He's not like our parents. When we mess up, I see God lovingly responding to us with, "Wow. I'm sorry you feel you failed, Daughter and Son. I'm sorry you messed up. I know you're hurting. It wasn't my desire for you to be hurting so much. I didn't want you to go through betrayal. I attempted to warn you. I didn't want you to be lied to. I gave you hints on how to avoid it. But you continued along your own way." Getting alone with Him, spending time with Him and allowing Him to saturate you with His Truth — with His Person, His character, the fruit of Who He is and what He did — this is what allows us to live freely. Freely. It is about Him respecting us and us respecting Him.

Maybe you're thinking, "Why would you want to talk about God respecting us?" I think it's important. Many people don't know God. They know only religion. They know only what they've been told. They know only what the preacher said. They know only what the teacher taught them. They only remember their mom or dad scaring them into relationship with the God Who would send them to hell unless they changed their sinful ways. They don't know personally what God thinks about them. They know only what others have said He thinks, and let me tell you something. You need to know what God thinks about you. He's not thinking evil thoughts. God is not sitting and thinking evil, malicious thoughts. The One Who lives inside of us does not think ill of us. You get it? The One Who lives within us does not think ill of us. He guides and leads us into all truth. And all Truth is a Person. It's not just a doctrine. It's not just a principle. Truth is a Person.

VALUE YOURSELF

I want to encourage you to pick up fresh value for yourself today. God created everything; He lives inside you and values you. Creator God lives within you and respects you. Your respect for yourself is a very important characteristic. When you respect you, other people are going to respect you. When other people respect you, you're going to have an open window in their lives to have conversation and be a real person with them. You will get to love them in a way nobody else can love them. And listen, people will mess up. Just love them. Because you know what? We also mess up, and we also need the love of God. We are not perfect. We do err at times. Sometimes we turn left when God really wanted us to turn right. What is beautiful about God is that when you turn right it still eventually turns to the left, and left still turns to the right. Listen — wherever we go, there we are. God is watching over us, watching over His Word to perform it and to help us live life with Him. He turns our wrongs into U-turns and leads us right back to Him. It's personal. It's give and take. It's an exchanged life.

I want to bless you today. I want to encourage you again to read **Acts Chapter 7**. I want you to see what

Stephen said. Look at what he was accused of. Look at how they responded to him. Look at how he was willing to say yes. You know what? I wonder about his private thoughts ... Did Stephen even know when he opened his mouth that he might pay the price of his life? I wonder if he knew.

Now on this side of the cross, a couple of thousand years later, I wonder how often we avoid saying the truth for fear of being criticized or disliked. Have we trained ourselves to be politically correct, and now we are cautious of speaking up for fear of a lawsuit or conflict? These are realities now, aren't they? Yet God is the same today as He was then and can still be trusted as we live in His Truth. Let's trust Him when we speak the truth and let's trust Him with the results.

BE STRENGTHENED

Be strengthened today. Be strengthened by the Word of God. Be strengthened by the words from God. Be strengthened by the One Who lives within you. God has nothing but respect for us, and we see it in how He gave us free will. And we, in turn, respect Him. Because He's our Father, He's a good Father, and He has nothing but good for us. We get to follow Him through a personal relationship with His Son Jesus by the power of the Holy Spirit. This same power is the same Spirit that raised Jesus from the dead. So resurrection power lives within us. It is still amazing, and it is still powerful. God trusts us to walk out life with Him. I love it. God knows the beginning from the end and back to the beginning. God's not afraid. God's not afraid of our messing up. God's not afraid of our mistakes. He's a good Father.

MISTAKES ARE INEVITABLE

How about if you and I decide not to be so afraid of our mistakes either? A mistake is not sin. We all make them. Let's take it one step further and choose not to be so disappointed with our errors that we are afraid to step out and make some more mistakes. Success is continuing to move toward the goal without giving up. Every bold action is an opportunity to move forward even in the midst of not always doing everything perfectly.

PRAYING FOR YOU

Father, I pray Your people will receive respect for themselves. I pray for them to rise in their value and see from Your perspective. I release a fresh insight as they see You living inside them instead of some unreachable god in the sky.

SPEAKING TO YOU

You are valuable. You are strong. You are more than able to look yourself in the mirror with respect and dignity. I release you to receive a fresh dignity for yourself. I release you to appreciate you in Jesus' name.

LOVE YOURSELF LIST

I want you to think of five ways you can respect yourself this week. Let these ways you choose be personal and possibly very private. Think of areas in your life where you have allowed yourself to be manipulated, controlled, abused or disrespected. On the other hand, I ask you a strong question — are you a manipulator? Are you the one who feels safe only if everyone is controlled by you? Are you the one verbally or nonverbally abusing others? Do you disrespect others?

Perhaps this is a time when you can look yourself in the mirror and have a good talk with yourself. It is critical to your growth and will aid you in your personal peace when you have a proper assessment and value of yourself. Since you were made in God's eyes, just know it is good for you to see yourself as significant and important. It is important to see yourself through righteousness and determine if you are behaving unrighteously. It may be time to make some changes.

You are the most significant person in your private circle. You have something to give back to society.

Write down the ways you want to respect you, and write down ideas that you can take action in. Maybe one way you respect yourself this week is by not disrespecting others.

1.

2.

3.

4.

5.

Respect actions:

1.

2.

3.

DAY 11. LOVE IS PATIENT

It is love that causes us to be patient and kind to one another. It is love that nudges us to wait for someone who is slowing down our pace. Maybe he or she is slower so we can learn how to wait patiently. When we can wait on purpose with a good attitude, we demonstrate a respect for a child's handicap or for an adult senior whose mind is no longer what it used to be. Just as God calls us to wait on Him, I believe He asks us to wait on others with respect and kindness. But how do you cultivate this kind of patience? Start by being patient with yourself and with others.

My Mind — Authentic love is steady. Love is pure with its intention. Love does not wish ill on others. Love is not harsh. God is love, and this is Who lives in me.

My Mouth — I am inspired by God's love for me. I am devoted to His love. God loves me and lives inside me. I can love myself with His love. I am patient with myself. I am steady. I am tolerant of my weaknesses and shortcomings. I am not harsh or unable to understand myself. I am not overbearing or flippant. I practice endurance with and for myself. I am for me — not against me. I am kind, confident and humble.

My Move — Today I am writing an uplifting letter about how I value myself. I am going to talk about 1) how I value my own abilities (what I do well) and 2) my positive/intangible qualities such as character. I will read it aloud to myself another day too, and encourage myself again and again.

Reflection Time

Did I write a letter about my abilities and character? I *do* have many things I can talk about. I am going to think about something I do well. I refuse to ignore my positive traits. What do I do well? *Write it down now.*

Examples of abilities and character: I might change diapers, run a company, be a caregiver for the elderly, drive a cab, cook incredible meals or be a clerk, pastor, friend or teacher. I might be patient and kind or loving and filled with joy. I might be an incredible listener.

Was it difficult to write a letter about me? Did I mention what I do, as well as something I appreciate about my character?

What was my experience (how I felt) as I wrote it?

Was I honest when I wrote it? Why or why not?

Spend 10 minutes in praise & 10 minutes in prayer.

Optional Reading — 1 Corinthians 13:4 NLT Love is patient and kind. Love is not jealous or boastful or proud.

Consider this: Respect for myself will cause me to recognize when guilt or condemnation want to have their way with me. Respect for His words about me will cause me to reject anything except what He says. When I love myself and am kind to myself, I am showing respect for myself. When I refuse to be jealous about others' abilities or special privileges, I am showing love for them and respecting them. When I refuse to boast or be arrogant about myself or others, I am showing love for me. When I love me, I am respecting me too.

DAY 12. FREE FROM GUILT

If I will learn to give myself respect, then I'll also have a heads up when my perspective is from a place of condemnation. The key to my freedom is to know His heart for me. Then, when words that reject His truth come to me or from me, I can reject them quickly.

My Mind — I am free from guilt and condemnation. God lives inside me, and He paid the price for my sins. So if God is for me, how can I be against me?

What came to me after reading about my freedom?

My Mouth — If God lives *within*, His presence inside trumps all negativity, guilt, condemnation and wrongs. I remind myself again that I am filled with forgiveness, and I am forgiving. I am kind and filled with compassion for others and myself.

My Move — I am going to tackle one thing I have been dreading or putting off. Perhaps I need to contact an old friend I've lost contact with, organize my workbench, clean my pantry or refrigerator, fix a leaky faucet or do outdoor landscaping. After I take action, I'm going to look myself in the mirror and say, "Good job!" I am not going to say anything negative to myself or about what I complete. I will say, *"Good job! I'm pleased with you!"* Now I will repeat it again with resolve in my voice. I will high five the wall right now! Can I easily say, "I'm pleased with me" or not?

Reflection Time

Was I able to be positive regarding me? Do I have a barrier to being kind or receiving kindness? If so, what is it?

Spend 10 minutes in praise & 10 minutes in prayer.

Optional Reading — Romans 2:4 TPT Do the riches of his extraordinary kindness make you take him for granted and despise him? Haven't you experienced how kind and understanding he has been to you? Don't mistake his tolerance for acceptance. Do you realize that all the wealth of his extravagant kindness is meant to melt your heart and lead you into repentance?

Consider this: I want you to know God is pleased with you. He's not mad at you. He loves you. He's for you. He's not against you. Some things are not your fault. Sometimes you might wonder, "How did this or that happen?" Sometimes years of actions are in motion; and then you change and you're a different person, but that thing is still in motion. Listen, God's going to free you. And it's going to be OK because He loves you. You are free to be free from guilt and to respect you.

DAY 13. SPEAKING TRUTH

Speaking the truth in love and rejoicing with God when the truth comes forth is an avenue of respect for yourself and those around you. Truth is powerful and can break through lies that want you to disrespect yourself or others.

My Mind — **1 Corinthians 13:6 NLT** It [Love] does not rejoice about injustice but rejoices whenever the truth wins out.

My Mouth — I do not rejoice when injustice takes place, and I do not behave unjustly. I want justice for myself, but I also want it for others. When unrighteousness seems to have the upper hand, I desire for righteousness to win. I dance for joy when truth prevails, and I love for truth to prevail inside me.

My Move — Today is my opportunity to speak the truth to myself. So aloud I remind myself right now, "I am loved and I am worthy. I am a child of God, a son/daughter of the King and the Truth of His kingdom lives inside me. I come from royal blood, and I celebrate how good Truth is in me. This Truth — I am made in God's image, I have worth and I am loved — is truth making me free."

Reflection Time

Do I believe I am loved? Lovely?

Do I believe I am rejected or respected? Do I reject or respect myself?

Read **Psalm 139:13-17** aloud. If possible, read from *The Passion Translation* and the *Amplified Bible* for variety. This section of verses shares how God Himself made us inside of our mother's womb. He talks about how precious we are to Him. It is personal and relational.

Does my worldview of myself agree with this psalm? The Word of God is the only template that will make me free — no self-help book can truly help me change the way I see me.

Spend 10 minutes in praise & 10 minutes in prayer.

Optional Reading — **1 Corinthians 13:7** Love bears all things, believes all things, hopes all things, endures all things.

John 8:32 ESV And you will know the truth and the truth will set you free.

Consider this: I want to reiterate that Truth is a Person. Allowing even a little lie into your heart can permeate what you believe about yourself, others and even God. So, what if you lived as if Truth and Love lived inside you? Allow the Person of Truth and Love become steadfast in you. Think what is true and lovely toward yourself. Let His truth make you free to believe and trust in yourself. Let Truth prevail in your relationship with God and with yourself. Feeling worthy is Truth. Feeling valuable is Truth. Feeling loved is Truth. Feeling significant is Truth. We allow our emotions to rule our lives so much that we base how we live on how we feel. Most of the time, our emotions contradict Truth. Let Truth contradict your emotions until your emotions are uncomfortable with feeling anything other than what is true.

DAY 14. I VALUE MYSELF

Valuing yourself is appreciating and respecting how God made you. It is powerful when we agree with God that what He did is good. When we value ourselves, others will value us as well.

My Mind — I value myself. I am going to consider this very thoroughly. Do I? What comes to mind?

My Mouth — I have an inheritance in love. God loved me so much He gave His very best — His only Son. God values me. If God values me by paying such a high price, surely I can value myself as well.

My Move — *Refer to my Love Yourself List.*

Reflection Time

How do I value or not value me? *Write down specifics.*

What came to mind when I read about valuing me? Have I ever considered God, as my Father, giving me an inheritance?
What *idea* did I incorporate into my life today?

Spend 10 minutes in praise & 10 minutes in prayer.

Optional Reading — **Psalm 46:10**

Consider this: I spent years not believing in me and not having value for myself — and the more

I devalued myself, the more people mistreated me. And the more I didn't love myself, the more I attracted people who didn't love themselves. It is not a stretch to understand that they didn't love me either. I attracted abuse. I'm not saying that's always the case, but that was the case with me. As I grew out of disvaluing and dishonoring myself, and I learned how to love myself, I attracted people who had a better value for themselves and for me.

DAY 15. I RESPECT MYSELF

When our actions are motivated out of love instead of self, then respect for God is shown, and respect for yourself is evident. His love and His respect will flow through you to those around you.

My Mind — **1 Corinthians 16:4 NASB** Let all that you do be done in love.

My Mouth — I have decided everything I do is out of His love for me and His love flowing to me. It's not enough for me to love others — I also need to love me. So I choose this day to truly grab hold of God's love. He has a pure intention toward me, and the love inside me is inspired by God's love. I am authentic and valuable in His love.

My Move — Today I want to show value for myself. I want a tangible expression of God's love for me. I will take a nap in the middle of the day, take a drive/ride, spend time at a store, listen to music or see a movie. I will do something unusual so it is a memory *with God* instead of just time out and about. I choose to enjoy relationship with Christ in the world He has given me.

Reflection Time

What did I do to feel God's pleasure for me? Was it awkward? Did I feel special? Am I authentic in my relationship with myself and with God?

Spend 10 minutes in praise & 10 minutes in prayer.

Optional Reading — 1 Corinthians 16:4

Consider this: If you do not think well of yourself, chances are others will treat you unkindly. When you allow disrespect to flow through you, it is possible that disrespect will also be given to you. Is this your life? How can you change?

RESPECT TAKEAWAY

You are free from guilt and condemnation.

You are commissioned to respect yourself.

You speak the truth in love to yourself.

You rejoice in the truth. You rejoice in righteousness. You love you. You value you.

You value others. You appreciate how you are made.

You think good thoughts about yourself. You forgive yourself.

You give yourself freedom to make mistakes and recover from error.

You choose life, love and living. You bless yourself.

You do it. For you.

CHALLENGE 4

I AM ACTIVATED

TEACHING — ARE YOU ACTIVATED?

Sometimes we need to take action instead of being passive in areas that are difficult to face. At times we encounter situations with our health, employment or family in which we need to make a new decision. It could be we need to take action in a relationship with a spouse, close friend or work partner. We must be activated in order to overcome.

AVOIDING CONFLICT

Action is where we get to grow. Honestly, it seems easier to avoid taking action in areas where conflict has arisen. But how can we grow without confrontation? Do you think that sometimes conflict comes in an area we feel we have no need to grow in? Maybe we feel our character is solid; and yet unbeknownst to us, we have compromise we need to address. When we avoid it, we don't get to mature in that area. Sometimes we're afraid to take action because we don't want to be rejected or to reject someone else, so we avoid it at all costs. That's not healthy either. Taking action is important.

DO IT AFRAID

As I was reading **Acts 9**, I thought about a disciple by the name of Ananias. He lived in the day when Saul encountered the LORD. Saul was blinded for three days in the presence of God. He was up close and personal with Christ, which caused him to make a change. Ananias didn't know about the new Saul turned Paul. No. All he knew about was the Saul who had been killing people. Personally, I would have been a bit fearful — what about you? God came to Ananias and said, "Look, I want you to go talk to Saul." Ananias was against the idea: "No way. Don't You know he kills people?" I love this about God. Some individuals think God wants only quick obedience and nothing more: "Do what I tell you to do!" On the other hand, some may feel God has done away with obedience. As a parent, however, I know my kids need to learn how to respect authority while also finding me to be a safe place to dialogue. I believe obedience is still part of an authentic relationship with God too. Interestingly, when Ananias questioned the Lord, He kindly explained, "Oh, but this is what's going to happen when Saul turns into Paul. This is how it's going to impact his life. This is what he's going to do with his life." The result of God's explanation was that Ananias went forward and did what the Lord wanted him to do.

LONG-TERM RELATIONSHIPS

I've often pondered about the encounter with Ananias and God. The Scriptures don't go into the nitty-gritty details, but I've wondered if this was the first time Ananias had met Paul personally. Did they continue relationship with each other? It doesn't really say if they continued, but you know those communities were close knit. What if every time Paul came into town after that, he got to talk with Ananias? What if they became good friends? What if Ananias was someone he conferred with and talked with, and he was an actual friend with him? What if that was just the beginning of a friendship? I love the thought that believers were in community as they worked out their new identities.

MATURITY

Believers were instructed to "Greet one another with a holy kiss" in the following Scripture references: **2 Corinthians 13:12; 1 Thessalonians 5:26** and **Romans 16:16**. Why did they greet one another with a holy kiss? We barely say, "Hi. How are you doing?" We barely shake hands. We barely hug. But you know why they greeted one another with such intimacy? I personally believe it was because they knew tomorrow may not come for some of them. They knew the next day might be the last day they would see their brother, sister, mother, father or friend. They knew their lives were truly at stake at all times, because they were ushering in what Jesus had come and done on the cross. They knew they were introducing the power of Holy Spirit to this entire community and on to the ends of the earth.

Ananias took action, and look what Paul did with it. He took action. And you know what? Our lives are no less important. Maybe you need to be activated in an area. When my clients and I meet to talk about an issue and that issue is resolved, I encourage them to consider their next steps. I implore, "OK, what are you going to do? How are you going to take action in that area to promote the change you have moved forward into?"

LOOK AT YOUR LIFE

Stop and look at your life. Where have you felt led to move forward? Maybe you need to say *no* to something. Maybe you need to say *yes* to something. Maybe you simply need to talk it out with a friend or coworker and come to a fresh conclusion. If you need to discuss a disagreement or uncomfortable situation regarding friendship, things can get sticky. So I'm not referring to severing relationships without discussion. That's not maturity. That's not love. That's not community. That's just a place of not forgiving. I want you to take action in your life and allow growth from God. Sometimes conflict is the very thing we need in order to grow and mature in a specific area, so that we can handle our future responsibly. Avoiding action might paralyze us or cause us to move so slowly that we procrastinate habitually and never change.

TAKE ACTION

I just want to encourage you today to take some action. It's interesting. As I am writing, this is the holiday season. Honestly, it's always a holiday season. There's a holiday or some sort of acknowledgement or day off every month. But in the specific times of Thanksgiving, Christmas and New Year's, suicide is high, depression is high and despair gets highlighted. There are all sorts of things that take place in this season with people who need some encouragement. Maybe you're the one who needs encouragement. In taking action, you may need to do something specific to protect yourself from thoughts, ideas, paranoia and voices in your head wanting to take you out of the picture entirely. It could be those ideas want to take you on a cruise you don't want to go on. Make a new decision, my friend. You are important.

ACTIONS IN RELATIONSHIPS

Take action in positive ways, not negative ways. You want to take action in community and in relationship with people. Don't sever relationships and walk away as if they don't have value. Listen, that's what we communicate with one another when we just cut off connection with friends or family we have loved. We sometimes feel God is nudging us to change our paradigms with others. We want to obey and know we must move forward in a specific pathway that includes family or community. So we cut people off and keep on going as if they won't miss us or we won't miss them. We think, "Well, I'm obeying the Lord." Really? Are you obeying the Lord, being unkind and rude? I know about this because I've done it before. My heart screamed, "I want to obey. I want to obey. I want to obey." Then I walked away without a discussion, not because of my obedience but because I was afraid of their response. You see? Fear was in charge of me. It is not always what we do but how we do it. I was not mature enough to demonstrate love as I was growing. I could have been kinder than my strict, legalistic obedience. God is kinder. I just did not know how to do it.

I love the way Ananias had the guts to go ahead and talk to Saul turned Paul. You know he was shaking in his boots. He was deathly afraid. Joyce Meyer says, "Just do it afraid." I want to encourage you to take action today, even if it's in an area you feel anxious. Whether it involves a relationship, a job situation, a community, a ministry, or life and death — believe again and take action. Maybe you've left behind believing in yourself or trusting God. Maybe you're beginning to move into despair. Take action. Move into trust. And if you don't know what joy looks like because you have been so down for so long, perhaps you need to get around somebody who smiles and laughs and is carefree. Don't allow yourself to remain in despair and depression. Take action. Don't wait for someone to take action for you. You take action. It's OK that you love yourself enough to take action regarding your own private misery. I release you to do it afraid. I release you to have mercy for yourself, to have compassion on yourself, and to love and value yourself enough to do something about your own life.

Obey the Lord. Not from a perspective of, "Oh my God. He's going to kill me if I don't obey Him," but from relationship with Him. He loves us, and anything He leads us into is for a purpose because He's so smart. Sometimes I see my clients restored long before they see themselves that way. I can see them whole because I know the One Who makes them well. So if you cannot muster up the courage to trust God, then muster up the courage to trust me. Do it afraid!

SPEAKING TO YOU

May you, dear one, take action to water that area in your life where you need to now live. May you take action to bring the nutrition it needs. May you take steps to thrive. If you see any weeds around it, may you pull up those weeds quickly. May you activate yourself so this plant will grow uninhibited and unhindered by weeds, thorns and rocks.

You are significant, and you are important. Don't you give up, and don't you turn around, because God is for you and not against you.

I love you and you are filled with the love of God. I give you permission to choose life for yourself right now.

PRAYING FOR YOU

Father, I pray for those who are strongly held in paralysis. They feel like there are shackles on their feet and they can't take action. We release them from those shackles. We break off what has kept them from taking action. We release those feet to move. We release that mouth from being mute. We release them to speak. We release those hands that have been tied and strongly held to addiction or self-inflicting pain. We break that off them because it is not who they really are. We sever that relationship with darkness and we release life. We release permission for them to live. God, I pray You will cause heaven to surround those who have such severe problems they feel their life is over. We release life. We release light. We release joy to come in. In my heart I see a plant sprouting up.

God, we agree, and we release water on the plant attempting to break through the soil and sprout up. It's a plant. It's not a weed. We release water so it will grow strong. Father, I pray as they water and feed themselves that You will bring them a harvest. Thank You that one day the plant will grow into a tree that will be covering and provide shade for others.

Live. Live. Live. Live.

SPEAKING TO YOU

Somebody reading this needs to take action in the area of life — of living. You are important. You have value. You are significant. You get to live. Maybe your circumstances suck. You know what? Sometimes they do for a season. But that doesn't mean you can't pass through this circumstance and get to the other side, and find an end or a solution to a problem that is desperate. I bless you today.

LOVE YOURSELF LIST

Pick five deeds for the week. Review and choose from these suggestions or do the daily suggestion.

- Do something you have been dreading. (This counts for two deeds.)
- Book a massage.
- Get a manicure/pedicure.
- Vacuum your car.
- Clean underneath your bed.
- Give yourself flowers.
- Look in the mirror, and tell yourself you like you.
- Compliment yourself or your clothes three times daily.
- Go out for coffee with yourself.
- Stay at home and enjoy a treat.
- Treat yourself to ice cream or a smoothie.

DAY 16. GOD IS MY FRIEND

Taking action is a powerful step in acknowledging your friendship with God. He talks to us as His friends, and His love lives in us and through us. God's love will help us like and love ourselves.

My Mind — God is my Friend. Is God real to me?

My Mouth — I have an inheritance in love. God's love lives inside me. It also flows through me. I'm a carrier of Love. I love myself because God loves me. I value myself because God values me. I like myself because God likes me. I enjoy spending time with myself because God enjoys spending time with me. We are friends.

My Move — Friendship is an interesting perspective to explore when it comes to God. Yet God says He is not only Lord, Savior, Master, Father, Brother and Parent, but also Friend.

Describe your personal thoughts on friendship with God. Talk with a friend.

Reflection Time

Is God truly my friend? Do I see how He desires to be my Friend? I will define why or why not. Do I value me? Am I learning to value and love myself? How? Am I growing in my own understanding and acceptance of His love and value for me? How?

Spend 10 minutes in praise & 10 minutes in prayer.

Optional Reading — John 15:15

Consider this: I want you to consider your friendship with God. It could be you don't feel you have one. Friendship is cultivated. We meet someone and say, "Hi. How are you doing?" Then we meet again and share a hug. Then we decide, "Let's get together." And then, "Let's have the family over." Then we suggest, "Let's go on vacation together." And then, "Let's celebrate birthdays." And all of a sudden, we're in the fabric of one another's lives. That's friendship. That's relationship turned into family. It's living out life with one another ... God lives inside of you. He's living out life with you. He's living life in you and through you. Whether you *feel* Him or not, He is there.

DAY 17. I TRUST GOD

As we decide to take action to trust Him, He gives us more and more of Himself, and He reveals more and more of Himself in a way we can understand and relate to. Then we can share this love with others.

My Mind — I trust God with me. I am taking a moment to imagine myself sitting in His hands. I'm closing my eyes and visualizing this now.

My Mouth — God has a pathway for me because He is interested in the particulars of my life. He loves me and has a plan for every season. When I am in winter, He knows how to keep me warm. When I am in famine, He knows how to get me food. When I am in summer, He knows how to bring me a cool drink. When I am in autumn, He shows me the colors of the new day. When I am in spring, He reveals new blooms and blossoms. I trust Father. When I am in darkness, He is Light for me. He gives me instructions so I can be in agreement with His will.

My Move — What do I want to do to show myself some love today?

Reflection Time

How can I trust God more? *Give specifics.*

I will recall a time when God took care of me. He may have protected my life or job, provided a need, etc. I will name one area of my life where I am struggling to trust Him as Father or Friend. I will surrender this area.

What *idea* did I choose today? How did this action affect my relationship with God?

Spend 10 minutes in praise & 10 minutes in prayer.

Optional Reading — Read some of your personal notes to yourself from your daily reading.

Consider this: Father God is completely and totally interested in you. His interest is not solely in your obedience. His interest is in how you relate to one another. Do you know Him? Will you let Him into your private world? Can you see His love for you? Difficult things come in life, but can you stop and see His goodness? Remember *He* is for you and not against you, and He says you are His favorite. So stop and rethink holding back from Him. Give Him all your heart. He in turn gives you all of His.

DAY 18. I FIND HIS GOODNESS

The goodness of God is found throughout Scripture; however, we do not always find it due to our own past hurts. Let's press past our pain and look for His perspective.

My Mind — God is good inside me.

My Mouth — God has good planned for my life. His plans for me are always for good and not evil, for success and not failure; and for a hope with benefits, security, welfare and peace. His goodness leads me into a change of mind.

My Move — I'm going to write my thoughts on Your goodness, God. Through thick and thin, You walk with me. You are persistent. You are relentless. Thank You for pursuing me and pursuing our relationship. I love You. Show me how to love You. Show me what devotion looks like.

Reflection Time

What are my thoughts on God's goodness? Can I see the faithfulness of Christ in my life and how He walks with me no matter the circumstances? Have I ever questioned His faithfulness? If so, when? What happened?

Spend 10 minutes in praise & 10 minutes in prayer.

Optional Reading — **Jeremiah 29:11 ESV** For I know the plans I have for you, declares the Lord, plans for welfare and not for evil, to give you a future and a hope.

Consider this: I was traveling recently. One day I was about to step onto a road, and someone suddenly pulled me back. It felt rough. But there was purpose in his quick movement. He kept me from getting run over by a taxi I hadn't seen. He had eyes to see what I could not see. He saved my life. Has God rescued or saved your life? Has God protected you from something? Maybe you felt like the scenario was harsh, but perhaps it was God Himself reaching through a person to help you. I want to encourage you in trusting God. Sometimes His ways really are not our ways. But God is on the job and He wants us to lean into Him. He wants us to believe He is for us even when we feel something has happened that is unfair or unjust.

DAY 19. I FOLLOW GOD

We can follow God only through His Holy Spirit. The Holy Spirit's job is to lead us into Truth. Truth is Jesus Christ. That being said, it makes sense that we follow God through our relationship with Christ. God is more than an untouchable deity — He is our Father. Understanding how a good Father directs us is different from a God up in the sky Who does not know us.

My Mind — I follow God.

Can I see how I follow God?

My Mouth — Father God directs my decisions and governs my heart with His ways and His thoughts when I surrender my life to Him. He puts desires in me so I can live my days following Him instead of empty pursuits. God has awakened my soul and brought me into a new morning.

My Move — I'm going pick up a mirror and look into my eyes. I am going to stare into my own eyes for a solid minute. I will say aloud, "I see You, Father God." Then I'm going to look into my eyes for an additional 60 seconds. I'm looking past me into the One Who created me.

Reflection Time

Does God govern my decisions? How? I am reading **John 15:4-11**. Do I struggle with knowing God's will? According to this chapter, how can I know God's will? What does *abide* mean? What is the warning in **John 15:4**? What is God's desire for me in **John 15:11**? Do I have barriers that keep me from abiding in God? If so, I want to stop now, talk to Him and listen to Him about it.

Spend 10 minutes in praise & 10 minutes in prayer.

Optional Reading — **John 15**, any translation. This chapter is about living in Christ and finding your identity in Him.

Consider this: He's taking action in your private world. He's pursuing you. He's not ignoring you. He's all in. I encourage you to ask Him to show you how to follow Him. I remember a few times when I felt as if my world was falling apart, and a close friend would say, "Tomorrow's a new day. The sun is going to come up — and it's going to be a new day." This encouraged me to look for God. I encourage you to take time to watch the sun come up or go down. See the beauty of creation. Remember you are made in His image and He is watching the sun with you. Consider how you follow God.

DAY 20. I AM SUCCESSFUL

Our Father God is for us. He is a good Father. He sees our weaknesses and strengths and works with us. He does not put pressure on us to be someone we are not. Success in His eyes is different from what we think. When you move forward without giving up, and when you continue to do your best but still don't get it quite *right,* it's not failure. Success to God is trusting Him as you do your very best along the way.

My Mind — I am successful.

What comes to my mind after I read the above sentence? Do I have a measuring stick for success that may not be His way of measuring it?

My Mouth — I am a new person. When I was still selfish and full of me, God died for me. When I was unaware of His Love, God died for me. When Jesus died for me, He set me up for success and victory. When Christ confronted death for me, I became dead to the wrongs of my life and alive to His life. He trumped all my wrongs.

My Move — I am going to fulfill a previous goal I did not accomplish. Have I received the victory Christ accomplished? Do I see His success operating in me?

Reflection Time

I walk in newness of life. God has made me new. I am successful because He lives inside me, and He is successful.

Spend 10 minutes in praise & 10 minutes in prayer.

Optional Reading — Romans 6:4 TPT Sharing in His death by our baptism means we were co-buried and entombed with Him, so that when the Father's glory raised Christ from the dead, we were also raised with Him. We have been co-resurrected with Him so that we could be empowered to walk in the freshness of His new life.

Consider this: I think that's the challenge for us — to see one another and to see ourselves no less than how Christ sees us — to see ourselves as already successful. I think when we see ourselves as winning, maybe we'll actually become successful in specific areas of past failure. In the meantime, we've got to believe in ourselves. We've got to rock on, people. Just walk on, rock on, and do the best you can with who you are while on the way to where you're going.

ACTIVATED TAKEAWAY

Do you find His goodness in the land where you're living? Are you able to find His perspective? Are you looking at the negative? Are you disillusioned often?

Reach past your emotions into the perspective of Father, and look to Him for guidance.

Find good in the bad. Find good in the ugly. Find good in the betrayal and disillusionment. Find something good where you're discouraged.

Reach through your feelings into His perspective, and find a new attitude. Don't let your anguish-filled emotions plant destruction toward God. Don't let it happen. Stop now, and recalibrate His goodness in you and your circumstances. Let today be your personal change of mind. Make today the day you move from unbelief to belief.

CHALLENGE 5

I AM VICTORIOUS

TEACHING — VICTORIOUS PAST

We think we know ourselves. We are convinced we are faithful and loyal, and we would never go against anyone we love. This is true with us and was true with Peter. Peter was one of the disciples Jesus spent time with and loved until the end. Peter was bold, vivacious, and outspoken. In a dialogue with Jesus, Peter said he would follow Him and lay down his life for Him. Yet Jesus knew what was inside of Peter and told him he would actually deny Him — and indeed, Peter did that very thing. I've considered what it would have been like to be Peter and to have actually watched my Friend die in front of me ... and to have walked so closely with Him I felt I would do anything for Him. How disappointed Peter must have felt when faced with his own self — when he truly did deny Jesus. Wow.

THE PROCESS

In my own life, there have been experiences that have taken quite some time to process, to forgive others and ultimately to forgive myself. How long was it before Peter got victory over his own past? When did he stop beating himself up? There comes a time when we must exchange our lives for His, truly receive the forgiveness He has for us and go forward.

There is nothing that could be more troubling than to deny the Son of God. No matter what you have done, and no matter what has been done to you, this is the time to move into complete and full remittance — full forgiveness. *Remit*, in my own vernacular, means to live as if that person — or you — never wronged you.

Grab hold of Christ today. Forgive. Be forgiven. Move beyond the past and enter into the victory He finished for you.

Let's talk about being victorious. What if the conflict we face — the problem we have — is actually preparation to win in a very specific area? It could be preparation to help others. It could be preparation for an unknown circumstance we will face in our future.

Peter was very interesting. He said he was all in for Jesus, but Jesus knew he was not yet strong enough to stand up when confronted. Jesus told him, "Look, you're going to deny me." Peter's attitude was, "I'm not going to deny You. I'd never deny You." Yet Jesus was thinking about his future. He confronted Peter even before the betrayal with, "After you change your mind about that denial — after you see what you really did, after you get healed and whole, after you come face-to-face with you and what happened — the instructions are: Go and strengthen the people around you." That is what Peter did. That was Peter's life. He did betray Jesus. He did deny Him. He denied he knew Him. Then he did come to his senses and did strengthen those around him.

THE CONFLICT

I've been thinking about conflict and what it can produce. It should eventually strengthen us. First of all, let's talk about Peter. I bet Peter was overwhelmed with guilt. I bet he faced feeling deeply ashamed and strongly condemned. I bet he had trouble forgiving himself and letting it all go. I bet he felt hopeless and wondered if he would recover. Peter was just like you and me. God is so good. He healed Peter, who then did strengthen his community. He helped communities know God intimately. He released them from condemnation into new life. He could help people forgive themselves. He could help them not be ashamed. Also, Peter's ability to receive forgiveness strengthened him to move forward as a leader who changed the world. He moved forward into this mantle of courage and became a pillar for the community.

What if the very conflict you and I are in is the key to becoming a pillar of strength?

A few years ago, I experienced a couple of whammies. First, I faced what seemed to be intentional betrayal from someone important to me. It hit very hard. I didn't even know what had transpired until later. This incident impacted our spheres of influence, and I felt as if some lifelong friends were no more. Honestly, it took a couple of years to be healed of my own unforgiving heart toward those who seemed to be guilty. That's how hard it hit me. Then after that season, a very close friend who had loved me suddenly disappeared from my life. That also felt like betrayal. Double whammy. The family no longer pursued relationship with me. I thought, "What do I do with this, God?" Automatically, I wondered what had I done because it looked like I was a common denominator in both situations. I had trouble letting the betrayals go because I'm the forever friend. I'm all in. I'd known people who had been intentionally unkind, but I had forgiven and moved forward fairly easily. Not this time. I was confronted with minimal answers. Why did this person not want to go forward in life with me? Why wasn't forgiveness enough? I did not have any solutions that satisfied me. What I knew was the value that once existed for me had changed. We were no longer in community. In this change, it was clear I was not in that person's future.

So what do you do if you're faced with a conflict involving someone you're all in with, but he or she doesn't want to be all in with you? What if you do get to let it go? What if you do get to just walk forward without that person? What if that's OK? What if the world inside you where you believe everybody is supposed to live in harmony was just a season in life? What then? What if it's OK that you live without one another? Wow. What freedom to understand that maturity sometimes brings separation.

THE CHALLENGE

Now, what if you're in a situation in which your state of mind has been challenged? What if your emotions are just wrecking you, and your mental health is at stake? This is indeed what I faced when my emotions went down a pathway where I felt betrayed. What if you can come to a place of clarity earlier than later? Would your perspective change if you knew ahead of time that the challenge could be your bridge to wholeness? What if it's your choice?

What if, instead of turning in to the depression, you decide you have value and can make new choices? What if you find out why depression is your friend? What if you get really freed and healed, and then you help other people get freed and healed too? It does not matter the area of challenge. You can overcome.

STRENGTH IN DISGUISE

What if the very area you want to give up in is your strongest strength?

Peter had a big mouth. I have to admit that I probably have a big mouth too. However, what if the very weakness you have is honestly your very strength? I realize I have repeated myself, but it is on purpose. In the middle of all of this weakness, you have to let yourself be forgiven. You have to forgive yourself for your weaknesses. You have to work through the guilt and condemnation that continue to swallow you up and take you whole, and want to move you into despair and destroy your life.

What if you were in a situation with someone who threatened he would do away with himself, and you didn't heed, and he killed himself? Then you were faced with the aftermath, and you felt guilt and condemnation. What if you could have done something about it? These are real areas in real life that really happen to us. People make their own decisions, and no matter what advice you give them, ultimately they are still responsible for their own lives. I want to encourage you to let go of any pain connected with someone else's decision to commit suicide. It is time to go onward. You cannot change it, and you must live. Also, I want to encourage you not to run away from your own weaknesses. Our weaknesses point us to His strength. So do not be down on yourself for your weaknesses, because they might be the very areas of strength you're called to and going to whoop butt in one day.

FROM SHUT DOWN TO GET MOVING

Sometimes my clients and friends have areas in which they shut down. Can I give you an example of shutting down? Imagine yourself in a car right now. The car literally shuts down, and you're not moving. Can you see it? Does it feel familiar?

What if mentally and emotionally, you have areas in your life in which you shut down? You sense *that* feeling is attached to something from your past. You may have no idea where that feeling comes from but it comes in your world. What if this area where you shut down is actually an area you're going to be victorious in? I want to tell you something. Don't give up on you. Don't turn back on you. Don't tune in to the voices that tell you you're a failure, you're an idiot, you're never going to make it, you might as well do away with yourself, you're not doing any good, or your contribution is not significant enough to matter. All of those voices, all of those thoughts, all of those ideas that are coming in between your ears — those are lies. They're not from the voice of authority. Those are from voices of unbelief that want to make you powerless in your life and eat your lunch. So let's decide today that you are not going to let that happen. Today is the day to change that channel. All right?

CHOOSING

Possibly, you have an ongoing difference of opinion with someone. Maybe you wake up in the middle of the night worrying. Maybe it's a need for a job. Maybe you're lonely. Maybe you are physically unwell. Maybe you're emotionally unhealthy. Maybe you have been betrayed to the point where you don't want to have contact with another human being. Maybe you have had people you trust turn away from you and leave you in the dust. Maybe darkness has called your name so long that you forget darkness is not your friend.

I encourage you to view the very area you feel weak in as an area in which you may be called to become strong. I can almost guarantee this conflict can be a position of strength. You get to choose how you respond to this messy place in life.

Listen. I am not saying, "You just choose by your will." I used to be the person who said you just do it regardless of how you feel. However, it is not always from our will alone. Because the emotions can be so strong, at times you do have to make solid decisions that make way for maturity and stability. You do get to decide, "I'm not going to hit that kid," or, "I'm not going to slam into that person who made me mad on the road," or, "I'm not going to shoot the finger at that person." I'm just getting real. At times you just have to choose not to let your own emotions rob you. Listen. You are empowered by God Himself inside you. That is where the choice comes from. The choice to say no is from deep within, and it's an empowerment to say, *no*. It's not just, "Oh, it's just my will. As an act of my will, I just say no." No. We all need Holy Spirit to help us because the soul can be strong. There is Someone living inside you Who has empowered you to give a righteous "no" — and empowered you to give a "yes" to what is righteous, to the more mature pathway forward.

The strength of God allows you to learn how to be victorious over conflict in the soul's realm.

WEAKNESSES

An area I've had issues and weaknesses with ... I'll just be honest ... has been sugar. I know. I said the *s* word. I used to hate coffee. I bet you coffee drinkers are thinking, "Really? What's wrong with you?" But I used to not like it. A couple of years ago, I started drinking coffee. Then I started putting sugar in it. Then I moved from half and half to creamer to honey. And then I moved to some of those fancy sugars like hazelnut, French vanilla and things of that nature. Sugar is not good for me. It causes me not to think straight. It causes me not to sleep right. It causes my elbows and knees to hurt. It causes me to have physical issues. I realized recently that it's an area of strong weakness in me. Maybe it wasn't a weakness in the beginning, but it has turned into one because I have ignored it. Starting now, I'm going to begin curtailing my sugar intake ... because I don't want to hurt, I don't want to feel foggy and I want to sleep at night. What if I take my own authority over my own body and negate eating an overdose of something that tastes good?

Do you have an area you need to work on in order to turn it from a place of weakness into a place of strength? Maybe you are dealing with offense. What if God has called you to be such a forgiver and to be so forgiven, and you ooze His love so much and so great, that you are the least offended person on the planet? What if you're the one the enemy comes to, and God says, "Nope — you can't touch her, because you can't find anything inside her." What if that's really your true calling? It is attainable through the power of the Holy Spirit.

I want to encourage you today. Look at your conflict. Look at the place where you hurt the most, and ask God what His strategy is for you to be victorious in it so you can turn that place into strength.

PRAYING FOR YOU

God, I release strength where there's weakness. I release life where there's death. I release a loosening of shackles from around people's necks, where they feel they can't hear You and don't know what's going on anymore. I release confusion from them. Father, I release strength where there are weaknesses. I release people from conflicts that are killing them or eating them alive. I release strategies from heaven to meet them — to give them ideas for what to do, what to say and how to partner with You as they choose life. I release them from how they've always been, what they've always said and what they've always thought into Your thoughts for them today. God, I release the minds of men and women to hear a new thought from You and to move into it, so they will be victorious because of Christ living within them.

SPEAKING TO YOU

Sometimes we want to linger in the past. Sometimes the past is dear to us. However, the past is gone. We can't go back. Sometimes emotions hold us in a past cycle because it was so special. I understand. But listen to me. It's your new day and you have permission to move into a new day for you. Even the good can hold us back from the better. It is OK that you move forward out of the past and be victorious in your future. That is your assignment. Let me get real with you. I want you to ask yourself right now if you are holding onto anything from the past that has been keeping you from living your tomorrow. Let me give you some examples. Are you holding onto the pain that came through the death of a loved one, the emptiness that came through the divorce from your spouse, or the heartache that came from a betrayal? What if you are holding onto the good from a specific birthday, the encouragement that came in a season of darkness, or a life-changing relationship that ended? Or perhaps something else has come to mind. Let that place of utter devastation or success be so transformed that you can be someone else's strong comfort. Let your past be in the past, and let your future come forth.

Let this painful past be your platform to strength. Let the conflict turn into a strategy. Find the empowerment, grace, mercy and strength that already lives inside you to permanently refuse the lies from your past and agree to the Truth in your future. Yes, yes, yes to what He has for you. God is the smartest Person we know. He's got a plan, a purpose and ideas.

I bless you today. I pray you will know God is for you and not against you. Get still. Be still. Listen. Hear. Write it down. What if you find that you are angry with God for how your life has turned out? Release that anger today. Let that offense go. Let that pain go. Then listen some more. Hear some more. And write down some more. Know God's got a new thought for you. His thoughts are victorious because you have the mind of Christ.

LOVE YOURSELF LIST

Choose five. Write down five deeds you are going to do for yourself this week. Kindness is important for you.

- Pat yourself on the back three times.
- Shout your victories aloud.
- Hold your own hand and remind yourself you are strong.
- Remind yourself you are confident.
- Remind yourself you are equipped.
- Remind yourself you can face anything with your chin up and eyes open.
- Toast yourself.
- Go to a movie you want to see.
- Buy yourself a flower or a trinket.
- Take yourself out for a meal.
- Tackle the job of reorganizing a disorderly section of your home or work place.
- Compliment your clothes each day.
- Compliment your hair every day.
- Compliment a specific ability daily.
- Smile at yourself in the mirror daily.
- Compliment a character trait.
- Compliment your own personality.
- Believe in you.
- Tell yourself you appreciate yourself.
- Look deep into your eyes in the mirror and tell yourself, "I love you." Then do it again.

DAY 21. GOD'S AFFIRMATION

I picture a dad at the end of a swimming pool rooting me on to swim to him, even though it means I will have to swim from the shallow end all the way to the deep end. God affirms our journey to be brave and to step out and trust Him. Do we always end up with the results we think we should? No, but we have a good Father Who is calling us forward to trust Him instead of our results. He tells us to trust His victory on the cross with all our weaknesses. If we begin to drown, His hand will pull us up just like it did for Peter when he sank after walking on water.

My Mind — I love myself with love from God.

My Mouth — I am pleasant because of God's love inside me. I am nice to myself too. I do not fight to have my own way all of the time because I know God is for me, and I am for me. I do not have to prove who I am or that I have rights. I do not get upset when someone either gets on my nerves *or* tries to anger me. I refuse to condemn myself when I am wrong. It is OK to like myself and be nice to myself.

My Move — Today I am stepping out in trust. I am rising up to address today's challenge. I am intentionally going to say aloud, "I look sharp. Wow. I am impressed with how You made me. You could not have done better. I am a natural and look like You. I love myself. I love how You love me and made me. I am content in being Your creation. I appreciate myself, and I feel rejoicing and joy coming upon me."

Reflection Time

Was I able to speak affirmations?

Do I like how I see myself? What is a new perspective I can pick up for myself that will help me?

I will name one thing I believe or say to myself that keeps me in a box never to change. For example, "I will never get better at _____." "I will always have problems with _____."

Finally, what does Christ say about me as opposed to what I say about me?

Spend 10 minutes in praise & 10 minutes in prayer.

Optional Reading — Romans 12:1-2 NLT And so dear brothers and sisters, I plead with you to give your bodies to God because of all He has done for you. Let them be a living and holy sacrifice — the kind He will find acceptable. This is truly the way to worship Him. Don't copy the behavior and customs of this world, but let God transform you into a new person by changing the way you think. Then you will learn to know God's will for you, which is good and pleasing and perfect.

Consider this: What if today you are the most angry, offended person you know? Can you picture God, Who says you have the capacity to love yourself, be at peace and be unoffendable? Can you picture yourself forgiven? Can you see you as you want to be? Can you move forward with you? You are worth it. You are amazing. There is nobody just like you. You have been made unique and special.

DAY 22. ACCEPTING GOD'S LOVE

Many of us struggle to receive God's love. How on earth do we receive from a Person we do not see? It is a process learning how to live out life with our Father. One thing I have learned is that if I will receive how He made me, I will learn how to genuinely like and love me. This will enable me to receive more of His love and the love of others. Eventually, I will love others more too. It's an amazing circle of trust.

My Mind — 1 John 13:34 NASB A new commandment I give to you, that you love (*with a social and moral sense*)[4] one another <u>even as I have loved you</u>, that you also love one another.

My Mouth — Today I am convinced of God's love for me. You love me. I am totally strengthened by Your love for me and how You take care of me. Because You love me, I can love others.

My Move — I'm going to find a window I can look out of, and I'm going to ask God to give me a new perspective on myself. I am looking forward to genuinely liking and valuing myself. I'm connecting with how you genuinely love me. I am in process, and the process is filled with Your love. I am responding in my composition book with complete honesty. What do I see? How do I see me?

Reflection Time

I will write down thoughts on God's love for me.

This day could be like a scalpel going into a scarred wound. God is going deeper to make me free to love and be loved. He has purpose in exposing infection. He wants to create an avenue through community for me to receive His love, as well as to love others in a practical way. He wants me to be honest and transparent so I can be whole. He does not want me to keep thinking any old thoughts I want about myself. God is my Father. Regardless if I have a poor or a good perspective — it is only God's perspective that matters. God has designed me to be whole.

I will name one area where my view of myself is negative. This might be something I have dealt with privately for years. Do I shut off God's love in that place? Do I feel so unlovely that I think He will reject me? Would I change my mind if I knew God loves me in my weakness? I want to be open to loving myself and being loved by God.

God, I ask You to help me receive the process of becoming whole.

Spend 10 minutes in praise & 10 minutes in prayer.

Optional Reading — John 13:34 TPT So I give you now a new commandment; Love each other just as much as I have loved you.

Consider this: Today I was feeling strange. I lay on the floor listening to Him and to me. I listened to my heartbeat. I listened to my own breathing. I felt God's love through my beating heart. I'm breathing. My heart's beating. My blood is flowing. I can see, speak and hear. I realized that He is in my heart beating and blood flowing. He is why I see, speak and hear. He was in all my senses this day and I felt His love for me.

If you cannot physically do these things, then God shows you His love differently. His love is simple. Sometimes God shows us love in ways we don't even consider are from Him. For instance, the love referenced in **John 13:34** is a moral and social responsibility kind of love. In other words, He loves you because He made you, and He feels responsible for you.

So ask Him how He loves you. Let Him show you ways He has loved you when maybe you felt He abandoned you. I encourage you to open your eyes to see how He loves. I encourage you to take this love and remind yourself you are victorious over your past.

I want to discuss a practical kind of love for a moment. Your breath is His love. Your ability to brush your teeth or have someone else do it for you is His love for you. I have a friend who is homeless at times, and even the sidewalk she finds to lay down her head is God's love for her. I had a very close friend who lived in shelters. Those shelters were God's provision for her. Look around you. Can you see God's love for you? Maybe you have not thought about how God's love is in your life. Perhaps love does not look how you want, but it does not mean He has not or is not showing you His love.

DAY 23. I AM THANKFUL

Thankfulness is an interesting condition of the heart. He tells us in **Philippians 4** to rejoice in all things and to come to Him with thanksgiving. Wow. He told this to people who were in great persecution for their faith. I have a feeling if we will choose to be thankful regardless of our circumstances, we will hear His voice differently than when we are busy complaining. What do you think?

My Mind — My glass is full, not half empty. I choose to be thankful.

My Mouth — I am strong in the Lord and the power of His might. I am filled with light, I am filled with joy and I am filled with rejoicing. I am well able to look at life in a positive light instead of a negative one.

My Move — I am considering at least five things for which I can be thankful. In the midst of what does not make sense, I am turning to You, God — because You make sense, and You will make sense of my life as I continue to trust You.

I will write my thankful thoughts down.

Reflection Time

Have I had experiences that have clouded my ability to find expectancy in my day-to-day life? Has someone died prematurely? Has someone else been diagnosed with an illness? Has confusion stolen a friend?

Spend 10 minutes in praise & 10 minutes in prayer.

Optional Reading — Romans 8:35 TPT Who could ever separate us from the endless love of God's Anointed One? *Absolutely no one!* For nothing in the universe has the power to diminish his love toward us. Troubles, pressures, and problems are unable to come between us and heaven's love. What about persecutions, deprivations, dangers, and death threats? No, for they are all impotent to hinder omnipotent love.

Consider this: If you can be thankful in a time when your own thoughts are ungrateful (and you complain, moan and groan, murmur and gossip), you've got victory. When you can turn the thought from negative to thankful instead, you've got victory. Part of the victory God won for us is our ability to change our minds. We can learn how to look at life through His eyes instead of our own lens. We can come out of agreement with attitudes that steal from us, kill us, or destroy us. Complaining, moaning and groaning, gossiping, and murmuring are emotions assigned to destroy. So I want to encourage you today to have a thankful thought. Be grateful. Move forward. Be victorious. You can be victorious, because God is for you and not against you.

DAY 24. ACKNOWLEDGING JOY

There is a Scripture in **James** that literally means to command joy although it says to "count it all joy." This was written to men and women who were experiencing deep tribulation and persecution. Their lives were at risk to be taken any moment for their profession of faith. I want to encourage you to tell yourself to have joy. Tell yourself what to do today — have joy. This joy will enable you to persevere until you reach a different perspective. You are His, so have joy — even if it is just for you.

My Mind — 1 Corinthians 13:7 AMP Love bears all things [regardless of what comes], believes all things [looking for the best in each one], hopes all things [remaining steadfast during difficult times], endures all things [without weakening].

My Mouth — I love and respect myself, and I can bear up under anything that comes my way with the love, respect and strength of God within me. Instead of complaining about me, I am silent and content. I am committed to trusting that He has a plan that is good. My confident expectancy for myself does not fade. I will not give up on me. I have hope, and I am trusting God with my future. I will remain strong and persevere with a good attitude and without weakening.

My Move — Today I am going to be like King David, who was a man after God's own heart. I'm going to dance for joy at me — God's workmanship. I will go someplace where I can be alone if I don't want others watching. I will jump up and down a few times and say, "Thank You, Jesus." If I am unable to jump up and down, I will lift my heels or toes a few times saying, "Thank You!" I am choosing today to celebrate that God made me. He did not make a mistake making me. I am His treasure, and I am wonderfully fashioned and made in His image.

Reflection Time

Was I able to acknowledge how You made me?

Read this verse aloud. **2 Corinthians 5:17 TPT** Now, if anyone is enfolded into Christ, he has become an entirely new creation. All that is related to the old order has vanished. Behold, everything is fresh and new.

I am a new person. And if I am new because of what Father and Jesus did on my behalf, what is holding me back from acknowledging my value?

God loved me before I ever gave myself to His Son. His love for me is not based on how I see me, nor is this love based on how I see Him.

Spend 10 minutes in praise & 10 minutes in prayer.

Optional Reading — Colossians 3:10 TPT For you have acquired new creation life which is continually being renewed into the likeness of the One Who created you; giving you the full revelation of God.

Consider this: Do you remember Dorothy (in "The Wizard of Oz"), who clicked her heels and talked about how there's no place like home? Well, my home is God. Your home is God. And it's much greater than any earthly place. So today I want you to celebrate that Father made you and how He did not make a mistake designing you. Celebrate how you are His treasure, you are wonderfully shaped and you are made in His image. I want you to acknowledge yourself today as a person made in the image of our Father. And I want you to agree that you are filled with joy as you do it.

DAY 25. GOD'S GOODNESS

The writer in **Psalms 27:13 ESV** said, "I believe that I shall look upon the goodness of the LORD in the land of the living!" Do you believe in the goodness of God in the land where you are living? You are God's goodness for you, your family and those around you. Have you considered the impact you have on your own surroundings? You taste good to those around you because His love lives in you. He never fails. You bring the atmosphere of His Love wherever you go, and His love is a game changer.

My Mind — Pure love from God never fails ... and I can love myself with His purity.

My Mouth — My love and respect for myself will never fail. God's love inside me is for me and never fades. My love will remain because He lives in me. Love does not fail — Love continues in and through me. My trust in God will not fail. My confident expectation of my future in Christ will not fade. My love for myself remains. Love never fails. Father, Your love for me is unchanging, so my love for myself is unchanging. I love myself. Your love in me will never fail — and my love will never fade. Love never fails. Love never fails.

My Move — Today I am going to either make or purchase a special treat for myself, and I'm going to toast myself while I drink or eat.

Reflection Time

Did I treat myself? Have I ever considered how God's love never fails and how His love inside of me will not fail either? Do I feel brave? How about bold? Respectful? Action oriented? Am I victorious over my past and encouraging for myself? Why or why not?

Spend 10 minutes in praise & 10 minutes in prayer.

Optional Reading — 1 Corinthians 13:3 ESV If I give away all I have, and if I deliver up my body to be burned, but have not love, I gain nothing.

Consider this: God's goodness doesn't fail. God's goodness leads us to a change of mind. I encourage you today to think about the goodness of God through His love — so you can see yourself the way He sees you, love yourself the way He loves you, and move forward into all He has for you. Love never fails. His goodness will see you through every challenge, conflict and success.

VICTORIOUS TAKEAWAY

Conflict can challenge us in ways other problems do not. We each have an idea we cling to and we have a desire to be right. That strong opinion can bring us into tension with friends, family and ourselves. Sometimes we are trapped in an emotional cycle that we must rise above in order to experience the love of God. We feel weak when faced with the confusion or frustration that comes with a different opinion. Yet that stress may only be a place that needs to be clarified and strengthened. Perspective is everything. We have talked a lot about Peter and how he felt guilt, shame and condemnation after throwing Jesus under the bus with his denial. Did his emotions swirl around him as they do us until healing comes?

Take the challenge you are in and look at the situation from another angle. Find the value in conflict, even if it is ever so slight. Find the pearl. Find the wisdom. Find the truth. Find the love. Find the avenue of letting go when you want to cling to your right to be right. Find the humility of letting go when you cling to your right to be wrong. Emotions can literally ruin you if you let them. We never would have heard of Peter had he not allowed restoration in his emotions. Sometimes you experience healing as a process. Sometimes you receive a miracle. The bottom line is that we get to live life in Christ as we figure out our true identity in

Him. We get to take on the truth of Him being for us and with us as He matures our weaknesses.

Grow from the experience and you win.

CHALLENGE 6

I AM ENCOURAGEMENT

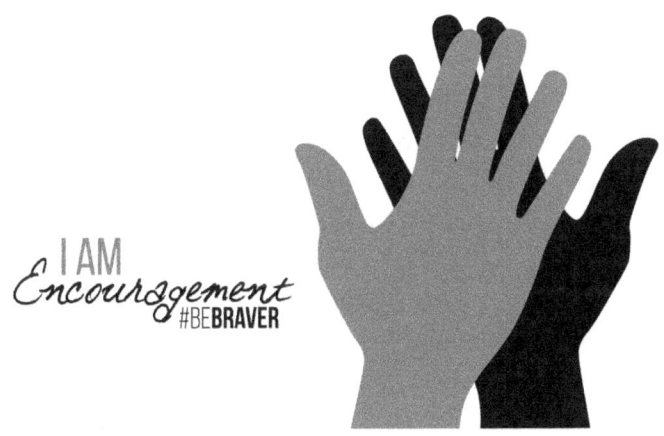

TEACHING — ENCOURAGE YOU

Beloved John was on the island of Patmos in Greece. Can you imagine being banished to an island because of your unwavering decision to trust God? Such was the case for John, who followed Jesus. Yes, Patmos was a place of amazing revelation. John, after all, wrote the book of **Revelation** — it is the Revelation of Jesus Christ. What did he do alone on the island? He was met with angelic visitation and encountered the living Christ. I do not know how long he was in His direct presence. After the encounter he was alone on the island without support or friendship. John was given the privilege of writing letters to seven churches (or communities) in Asia, to encourage them to be strong in the Lord as they faced persecution.

He had to have encouraged himself in the Lord. His enemies attempted to boil him in oil, and even that did not kill him[5]. So they moved him onto an island. He knew Christ in him, and he knew Holy Spirit and had His reality — true. But he was still a man who faced real life and death situations. John, a man given the responsibility and honor of loving and caring for Mary, the mother of Jesus, after His death — was still faced with being alone. How did he handle being alone? Did he remember times with the Savior? Did he pray all the time? Did he fish? No Internet, no cell phones, no movies or libraries existed. He was alone.

Have you ever been alone? There is a place in *alone* where you turn to God and receive all He is, all He has and all you are to become.

The Spirit lived inside John, and He lives inside you too. John experienced encounters and an visitation from the Lord Himself. But after the visitation was over, how did he feel? Was there silence? Did he *feel lonely*? I honestly do not know. Maybe he was silent. There may even be silence in Love when you encourage yourself in that Love.

ENCOURAGE YOURSELF

I believe Mary, the mother of Jesus, had to encourage herself many times. I'm sure she pondered how she had yielded her life to the will of God. I'm confident she also thought about the life chosen for her son. What a crossroads she must have faced. Think of how she experienced her own son giving Himself up on a cross. I encourage you today to grab hold of purpose in your pain or personal crossroads. Decide not to be discouraged, and move into a place inside yourself where you sense His love, approval, encouragement and acceptance.

PRAYING FOR YOU

I want you to pray for yourself this time. Talk to Father about yourself. He will guide you. He is for you and knows what you need, want and desire, even more than you do.

LOVE YOURSELF LIST

You have five good deeds to accomplish for yourself. Though you might be tempted to do them all in one day, I want you to spread them out and train yourself to receive kindness. Kindness is learned — not imparted. Remember, it is the impact of love or kindness you make on yourself that matters.

Review and choose what you want to do this week.

- Compliment your clothes at least five times daily.
- Compliment your hair two times daily.
- Compliment your abilities three times daily.
- Smile at yourself in the mirror three times daily.
- Compliment your character and personality five times minimum this week.
- Tell yourself you love yourself. Seriously. Do it.

DAY 26. MY PERSPECTIVE

In **Romans 8:1** you can experience a freedom like no other freedom. You no longer have to eat condemnation because Christ in you trumps all your past. Guilt is no longer your food. Look up and see Him, and know the Father and Son. Imagine His reality living inside you. Picture an apple core inside an apple. You are the apple and Christ is now your core. Think of it. You are alive because He lives in you.

My Mind — I refuse to allow myself to be condemned or guilt-ridden by my past, present or anything else.

My Mouth — I am free from my past and free from all guilt. I am a new person who can walk onward without looking back at the past as my template for life and living. My new template for living my life is His Words for me. I am willing to learn a new perspective for myself.

My Move — I am going to find a mirror, look myself in the eye and speak something outlandishly nice about myself.

Reflection Time

Do I have a new perspective about me?

Did I find guilt inside me? I let the guilt go.

Spend 10 minutes in praise & 10 minutes in prayer.

Optional Reading — Romans 8:1-2 The Message
With the arrival of Jesus, the Messiah, that fateful dilemma is resolved. Those who enter into Christ's being-here-for-us no longer have to live under a continuous, low lying black cloud. A new power is in operation. The Spirit of life in Christ, like a strong wind, has magnificently cleared the air, freeing you from a fated lifetime of brutal tyranny at the hands of sin and death.

Consider this: I just want to encourage you today to really grab hold of you being a new person — a new creature. Because what Jesus did, He did for everybody, including you and me. Let's include your neighbor who doesn't yet know God. Just because he or she hasn't experienced Him yet doesn't mean God did not already give His life for that person. So allow yourself to love people around you. Allow yourself to walk out life with no condemnation — for you or for those around you. There's great victory in that perspective. There's great encouragement in that perspective. You will be encouraged when condemnation doesn't rise to taunt you. You will see love in you when you see condemnation cease to rise through you to taunt others.

DAY 27. GOD LIVES IN ME

Understanding Father, Son and Holy Spirit live inside you is a revelation that will change your life forever. Christ made you alive. You are His, and you can choose Him. You are in union with Him and in Him, and you are never alone. When you see His presence in you, you can do all things He asks you to do, because you know He lives in you. You can have joy in the darkest hour when you are aware of His reality inside you.

My Mind — God lives in me.

Do I believe this reality?

My Mouth — I belong to God. God, You are my Father. What an inheritance I have in You. What a pleasure it is to belong to You. I am literally not alone. I host the Spirit of the Living God. How incomprehensible to think God is in me.

My Move — What intentional deed for myself comes to mind today? I'm writing it down now.

Reflection Time

How does God live through me?

Do I think differently knowing God lives in me? What is something I want changed about how I think?

Spend 10 minutes in praise & 10 minutes in prayer.

Optional Reading — No reading this time. Instead, repeat the following aloud:

I belong to God. God, You are my Father. What an inheritance I have in You. What a pleasure it is to belong to You. I am literally not alone. I host the Spirit of the Living God. How incomprehensible to think God is in me.

Consider this: Colossians discusses how the Godhead (Father, Son and Holy Spirit — all three) lives inside you and me. This is big. It is huge. It is mind blowing. It should make us whisper, "Whoa" and "Wow" all at one time. We are fully alive. You are alive, and I am alive. God lives in us. We breathe His very breath.

DAY 28. HOW GOD SEES ME

When you are born again, you have access to all He is inside you. You are His daughter — His son. You are forgiven. What would you do or how would you live if you saw yourself blameless? Wow. If you saw others innocent, would it affect how you treat them? How do you value others now?

My Mind — Philippians 4:8 NASB Finally, brethren, whatever is true, whatever is honorable, whatever is right, whatever is pure, whatever is lovely and whatever is of good repute, if there is any excellence — if anything worthy of praise, dwell on these things.

My Mouth — I see myself through the eyes of this Word, and I think thoughts only from His words about me. I release His truth deep inside myself. I think honorable and honest thoughts about my present, future and forever. I lean into His understanding and know He has made me innocent and pure. I am acceptable, and I am valuable. I am spoken well of, and I speak well of myself. I am a person of excellence, virtue and boldness. I can commend myself because God created me Himself, and God never makes mistakes.

My Move — Today I am going someplace quiet to consider His thoughts. I will be still for at least fifteen minutes or longer while I listen to some music uninterrupted by computers or people. I can meditate on this Scripture from **Philippians 4:8**.

Reflection Time

How long was my uninterrupted quiet time? What happened in the quiet? How do I recognize what is not characteristic of His goodness? Am I willing to have regularly scheduled, uninterrupted time with Him?

Spend 10 minutes in praise & 10 minutes in prayer.

Optional Reading — Philippians 4:6-7 NASB Be anxious for nothing, but in everything by prayer and supplication with thanksgiving let your requests be made known to God. And the peace of God, which surpasses all comprehension, will guard your hearts and your minds in Christ Jesus.

Consider this: You are seen through Love. He sees you forgiven and blameless. You didn't do anything for this condition. He forgave you before you responded, without your permission or help. He sees us as His children. He's your Father. He's my Father. He's your neighbor's Father. That's big. That's a game changer for me in how I treat people, how I see people and how I love people.

DAY 29. I AM SALT

Do you use salt? Salt is a preservative and is used to keep food longer to be eaten later. Salt is also used to make food taste better. If you and I are salt, God will preserve lives through us and make life taste good to those who live around us. Salt is powerful, and so are we.

My Mind — I am salt and I taste good.

My Mouth — I am full of life. Jesus says He is the Way, the Truth and the Life. Jesus says He is the salt of the earth. Jesus says He has peace no human can give us. Because Christ lives inside me, I am filled with His ways, His Truth and His life. I am also the salt of the earth. I live in tranquility because of the confident hope in Him that is in me.

My Move — I will eat something without salt and then salt it. Does that food taste better to me? Can I see how my life has changed because of God living inside me?

Reflection Time

How has God's life in me changed me? I will meditate on one way God's life in me has changed me. I will be specific.

Spend 10 minutes in praise & 10 minutes in prayer.

Optional Reading — Colossians 4:6 NASB Let your speech always be with grace, as though seasoned with salt, so that you will know how you should respond to each person.

Consider this: We are salt so let's behave like we taste good. Let's realize the goodness of God. I want you to treat yourself with grace. I want you to respond to yourself with life, mercy and kindness. When you mess up, blow it or say negative and faultfinding words, I want you to stop and visualize pouring salt onto yourself. You taste better now. Move on.

DAY 30. I FULFILL GOD'S PURPOSE

Everyone's purpose is different. God shows us how to live for Him with His ideas and abilities. When we are one with Him, we will know purpose as He leads us — even over a lifetime.

My Mind — I fulfill God's purpose.

What comes to my mind after reading the above?

My Mouth — I am more than a conqueror through Christ Jesus because His conquering Spirit lives in me. I can do all things He assigns to me because He is stronger than death and lives in me to complete His purpose.

My Move — I will hug myself. I will wrap my arms around myself and hug myself really tight. I will do this for at least a solid minute.

Reflection Time

How do I demonstrate His conquering Spirit?

How do I feel when I think about the conquering Spirit of Christ living in me?

I will find a small group of two or three people and discuss an area of my life that needs an infusion of

God's power. I will pray for myself and declare I will fulfill God's purpose.

Am I growing Bold? Respectful? Activated? Victorious? Encouraging?

Spend 10 minutes in praise & 10 minutes in prayer.

Optional Reading — Psalm 27:1 NASB The Lord is my light and my salvation; Whom shall I fear? The Lord is the defense of my life; Whom shall I dread?

Consider this: I want to encourage you in fulfilling God's purpose. Maybe you aren't where you think you should be. Maybe you have accomplished a great deal, and you feel satisfied and happy. Maybe you've got a bucket list. Maybe you're random in how you address a lot of things at once, and you wish you were more purposeful. Whatever the issue is, I encourage you to look to Him because He's the One Who bears fruit through us. And He really will accomplish His will through you if you continue to simply acknowledge Him and look for His response. Remind yourself not to fear. Remember He is for you. He is your light. Your pathway is lit and you can make good decisions. He is your defender.
You have no need to dread. Decide to expect again. Decide to have confidence again.

ENCOURAGEMENT TAKEAWAY

God Himself is alive inside you. You are one with Him. He is one with you. If you can truly capture this multi-faceted revelation, it will change you forever. Jesus paid the price for you to be alive. You are His, and you can choose Him.

In Him you are never alone. You can do all things He asks you to do. Discover Him living inside you. You are not doing anything alone. Once the lightbulb goes off, you can have joy in your darkest hour. How? Father, Son and Holy Spirit stepped inside you when you were born again. God lives in you. Talk about encouraging yourself *in* the Lord. This reality should change you. This means that whatever you face and whenever you face it, you do not face any of it by yourself.

CHALLENGE 7

I AM HOPE

TEACHING — HOPE'S EYES

Hope is an interesting phenomenon. Christ Himself is referred to as our living Hope. Hope is powerful. In the New Covenant, hope actually means confident expectancy.

A woman approached Jesus with an expensive bottle of perfume and poured the liquid on Him. It was a kind action to Jesus, Who was nearing His time to face the cross and move to heaven. Those around her felt if they had sold the perfume, the profit could have been used to benefit the poor. Interestingly, one of the people who felt the perfume was misused was a thief who usually stole money and who ultimately betrayed Jesus.

Sometimes our actions are not practical or logical. At times they make no sense to those around us or even to us. Yet on the inside, we know the action is significant and perhaps even a once-in-a-lifetime opportunity.

PERSPECTIVE

However, this woman named Mary Magdalene had a different way to see. Though the Scripture does not use the word *hope* in her context, her actions reflect a bold, confident expectancy — a reaching forward. She did this with her actions. She honored The One Who Died for the planet.

Think about it. A woman considered unclean by society's standards loved Jesus in a way no one else loved Him. She was in a room with disciples who thought poorly of her and probably wondered what business she had being that close to Jesus in the first place. Have you ever considered that perhaps those watching were jealous because they had not thought of a significant way to honor Him?

She had a perspective no one else had. Had He given her courage? Had He demonstrated an expectant heart just through being her Friend or being a voice that said, "You can do it"? Maybe He had been kind to her. Maybe He had spent time with her and caused her to have a better opinion of herself. Maybe she was growing in the love that could come only from the Father. All I know is, I see a woman changed so much by Him that her hope — her bold confidence, her bold action and her expectancy — is visible for the world to see. She went out of her way to give something no one else thought to give. And because of her actions, she is remembered; and her actions are honored as they are recorded in the most well-read book on the earth — the Bible. He is hope, and He gave her hope — a confident expectation and boldness.

LOVE IS THE ANSWER

Love is the answer. Love for others. Love for self. So allow Love to move you into a bold confidence in Him, in yourself and in the future He has for you.

Have you embraced the Love of God for you? How about this: Have you embraced the love of God for others? Do your actions have intent to honor? Have you a confidence and expectancy in Him?

Is your boldness something to be reckoned with, as hers was? How do you see you? How do you see others?

What do you see when someone around you thinks outside the box? Are you inside a box? Maybe it is time you step outside of limitations. Be expectant.

PRAYING FOR YOU

Father, give them eyes to see, ears to hear and a heart to comprehend who You have created them to be. Show them how to embrace Your love. Show them fresh actions to show themselves a new love. Take them outside of their box into Yours in Jesus' name.

LOVE YOURSELF LIST

You get to come up with five good deeds for you to accomplish for yourself this week. If you really want to be bold, how about coming up with five good deeds for your entire group to accomplish? Talk about it and determine if they're doable.

1.

2.

3.

4.

5.

Talk with Holy Spirit: What can you do to truly encourage yourself? Do you have expectancy for yourself? If not, what can you do to take a step toward becoming expectant?

DAY 31. LOVE OF CHRIST

Let God encourage you today. Look at His love and His affection for you, and treat yourself as kindly as you would someone else. Serve yourself as you would serve another. Let His love, resurrection and presence bring new strength in you and cause you to rise in bold confidence.

My Mind — **2 Corinthians 5:14-15 ESV** For the love of Christ controls us, because we have concluded this: that one has died for all, therefore all have died; and he died for all, that those who live might no longer live for themselves but for Him, who for their sake died and was raised.

My Mouth — God shows me love through charity, benevolence and affection. This love holds, strengthens and sustains me. Love gives me confidence. Not only did He die for me, but I also died with Him. This means I no longer live to protect myself with rules. Instead, I live in bold confidence. I was raised to life with Him. If I have already died — I can't die again. So I choose now to live by His Spirit as I move forward in bold expectancy.

My Move — I will hug myself multiple times at various times of the day. I might even set an alarm to remind me if I have a busy day ahead. I may feel awkward but it will be all right. So I put my arms around myself, close my eyes and intentionally receive more of Him and His love. This is the intention — to be loved. Can I show myself affection? This is important because we must be willing to demonstrate love for ourselves.

Reflection Time

How does the love of God control me? Do I show myself affection or benevolence?
Could I show myself affection by hugging myself? I am learning to hug myself regularly.

Spend 10 minutes in praise & 10 minutes in prayer.

Optional Reading — 2 Corinthians 5:14-15 For it is Christ's love that fuels our passion and motivates us, because we are absolutely convinced that he has given his life for all of us. This means all died with him, so that those who live should no longer live self-absorbed lives but lives that are poured out for him — the one Who died for us and now lives again.

Consider this: Adam condemned the whole planet with death; Jesus gave the whole planet life. That's huge. I'm telling you, I have not behaved free most of my life. But I'm learning. I'm picking up the reins in a different way. I'm receiving the love of God for me even more deeply than I have before. I'm moving forward with the love of God on me, in me and through me — because His love lives inside me.

DAY 32. LIKENESS OF GOD

When we are born again into the New Covenant, we receive a new self. The person we were is literally gone. This is your new day. Your past is over. Your new day in the new person called *you* is here.

My Mind — I truly can put on a new me because Love lives inside me. I am righteous and filled with truth. Wow. This is the real me.

My Mouth — Every day is a new day, but today is an especially new day. I am a new person. I sever the past from me. I sever my wrong thoughts, my wrong actions and my wrong ideas. God, I turn to You and say, "Here I am." I am made in the likeness of the Creator of the Universe. I am made like the King of Kings. I am made in His likeness. I am made righteous, holy and truth-filled.

My Move — I am sitting down with intention to think about how God loves me. I'm going to think about His love for at least five minutes — even if I set a timer. How am I a new person? *Write it down.*

Reflection Time

How does God reveal His love for me every day?

I am writing down one way God loved me today …

Spend 10 minutes in praise & 10 minutes in prayer.

Optional Reading — Ephesians 4:24 TPT And to be transformed as you embrace the glorious Christ within as your new life and live in union with him! For God has re-created you all over again in his perfect righteousness, and you now belong to him in the realm of true holiness.

Consider this: You are righteous, holy and filled with truth. You're a new person. You're not the same person you were yesterday. So make a decision today to live differently from how you did yesterday. If you didn't like how you lived, then change your mind and do something new today. Do something unique today. Make a change in your thoughts today. Look at yourself outside your own box today.

DAY 33. GOD LOVES ME

God does not just love the entire world — He also loves *you*. Be encouraged today because faith, hope and love live in you as God lives in you.

My Mind — **1 Corinthians 13:13 ESV** So now faith, hope, and love abide, these three; but the greatest of these is love.

My Mouth — I wear the clothing of trust, expectancy and love. Faith, hope and love live inside of me. My God persuades me. I rely on Christ for my rescue. I trust and am trustworthy. I trust my future to be divinely orchestrated. I am filled with joyful *hope*. I am confident for my future. God has a plan for me.

My Move — Today I am to sit in a chair or on the floor in quiet long enough to still my mind from busyness. God, You are good. You love me. I have to grab hold of this truth. My circumstances do not prove Your love. Your sacrifice and decision to live Your life for me are proof.

Reflection Time

What ways does God show His love and goodness for me?

How do I (or how do I not) abide in faith, hope and love? How long does it take me to become still and sense God?

In my quiet time, did I experience God's love for me? Have I ever thought about how very personal God's love is for me?

Spend 10 minutes in praise & 10 minutes in prayer.

Optional Reading — John 3:16 TPT For this is how much God loved the world — he gave his one and only, unique Son as a gift. So now everyone who believes in him will never perish but experience everlasting life.

Consider this: The Father and Son made an unbreakable agreement, and we get to experience this covenant. We have the opportunity to agree with what they have already accomplished. What has been accomplished, you might ask? Father and Son made a covenant with One Another — they ransomed our lives. Because of the actions of this unconditional love, you and I are forgiven and can forgive. You also have complete and total access to unconditional love for you and those around you. You have entrance into the love of God that never fails, never gives up and never quits. You are a whole new person. You now have truth living in you. You are alive. You are light. You have access to everything you need to move forward into the goodness of God in the land where you're living.

DAY 34. GOD GIVES ME LOVE

The Holy Spirit speaks to each of us through our mind, will, emotions and intellect. He permeates me and breaks all the religious rules. He loves us and shows us His love through every avenue we allow. I encourage you to let God lead you supernaturally so you can see how He is for you in your normal every day.

My Mind — Do I live and walk by the Spirit?

My Mouth — I live by His Holy Spirit. I am *in* the Spirit. I walk with Him, live with Him, run with Him and sit with Him. If I live by His Holy Spirit, then I desire my actions to be *hope* centered — bold, expectant and supernaturally led.

My Move — I am sitting and thinking about Love and how God has loved me. I will do this at least one time and for at least five minutes. I'll write a note about how He loves me. Then I'll either email or snail mail it to myself.

Reflection Time

How can I make decisions from love by His Spirit?

I will name three ways I have experienced the love of God since I began this study. Have I experienced His forgiveness? Have I forgiven someone else? Have I had answered prayer, or has someone been kind to me? How about a new revelation? Bravely, I will read my note to a friend.

Spend 10 minutes in praise & 10 minutes in prayer.

Optional Reading — Galatians 5:25 TPT We must live in the Holy Spirit and follow after him.

Consider this: In your day-to-day life, the supernatural or living by the Spirit is not ooky-spooky. Living by the Spirit can encompass practical things day by day. Are you living by the Holy Spirit? Are you in the Spirit? Living with Him? Running with Him? Sitting with Him? Hope-filled? Bold? Expectant? Encouraged? Active? Are your actions answering a supernatural call through practical life?

DAY 35. GOD'S TANGIBLE LOVE

It is not a myth that God sent His Son as us. Then the Son moved intentionally and took an unthinkable action to make His love known to us. His love was and still is tangible.

My Mind — **John 3:16 AMP** For God so [greatly] loved and dearly prized the world that He [even] gave His [One and] only begotten Son, so that whoever believes and trusts in Him [as Savior] shall not perish, but have eternal life.

The Passion Translation says it like this: For this is how much God loved the world — he gave his one and only, unique Son as a gift. So now everyone who believes in him will never perish but experience everlasting life.

My Mouth — I am so grateful God has a social and moral responsibility for me. He thought of me as His prize, so He sent His only Son for me. I choose this day to cling to Him. I trust in Him. I rely on Him. I give myself back to Him. I will not be destroyed, and I will not be led astray. I have a bright today, tomorrow and forever ahead of me.

My Move — Today I am going to buy myself an affordable, tangible gift for less than 20 dollars. This is to serve as a reminder to me of God's love. Every day is really Christmas when I understand the love of the Father through the Son.

Reflection Time

Do I truly *trust* and *believe God* loves me?

Jesus Christ is the greatest gift. Do I know that His love for me is why I can love me? He is living hope. I hold living hope in me. What gift did I buy myself? Was it significant and if so, how?

Spend 10 minutes in praise & 10 minutes in prayer.

Optional Reading — Read this passage again. **John 3:16 TPT** For this is how much God loved the world — he gave his one and only, unique Son as a gift. So now everyone who believes in him will never perish but experience everlasting life.

Consider this: Every day you can understand the love of the Father through the Son. Do you truly trust that Jesus died for you? That Christ now lives for you and inside you? That the Father loves you? If anything, I hope I have conveyed that it is all right for you to love yourself. I expect you to receive Father's love for you. I want you to give you permission to love you. Loving yourself will enable you to really, truly move forward in life. Loving yourself will increase your capacity to live and love others. Loving yourself will enable you to fulfill your purpose on the planet.

HOPE TAKEAWAY

When we are born again, we receive a new self through the amazing New Covenant. Do you know what Jesus did? He gave us a whole new life with all new possibilities. He gave us new strength. Perhaps we don't realize what we already have?

There's so much more than we allow ourselves to experience. This is your new day. Your new day in the new person called *you* is here. You're not the same person you were yesterday.

Make a decision today to live differently from how you did yesterday. If you didn't like how you lived yesterday, then be different. Expect change. Make a bold change in your thoughts. Look at yourself with confidence in the mirror and tell yourself, "I'm a new person who is bold, confident and expectant.

CHALLENGE 8

A BRAVE NEW ME

INTENTION — BRAVE NEW YOU

Recently, I have had to face some very difficult things about myself — some good, some bad and some ugly — and I'm having to choose how I want to move forward into a new me.

Moving into becoming a new you is not a name-and-claim-it type of thing. It is a declaration that you are ready to face a new future. Who you are to become is not about what you have said you are or are not, but rather what God says about you. When you read the Bible through and through, you realize it is filled with real people who faced common identity issues. We face these same problems today. What Jesus did for us on the cross gives us the strength and power to overcome any obstacle that prevents us from becoming a new person. Maybe you have spent a lifetime listening to naysayers, or maybe you have been your own naysayer — I don't know. But this is the day to let Love win for you and for your future. Time to believe in you and take action that proves it. This is your time to set a strong intention to a new you.

RESENTMENT, BITTERNESS, FEAR

Recently, I met a couple that got married two days before I was born. They were celebrating their 55th wedding anniversary the same weekend I was celebrating my 55th birthday. The wife was attempting to push her husband (who was in a manual wheelchair) through the doors and into the fresh air. I opened both doors for them and followed them outside. I offered to take their picture, and I took a number of photos for them with their own camera. She told me that on their 50th wedding anniversary, they were given a plaque with the words *resentment, bitterness* and *fear,* and underneath was the phrase Love always wins. Then she told me she really wanted to create a tapestry with that saying to hang on her wall. We chatted about how no one could be married that long unless love was winning. Her husband had a stroke, they moved in with their daughter and son-in-law — a completely different generation — and they were all having challenges. I shared with them how I thought it was God's blessing to the younger people that they see his and her resilience — that they see people who have chosen to stay married in covenant. I felt strongly that their daughter and son-in-law's lives would be changed by witnessing family who has chosen to remain together through thick and thin, through good times and bad times. I truly wanted this couple to see that they mattered and that they were an example of how love always wins. I asked the man if he enjoyed living there, and he said, "No." But of course, he'd had a stroke and didn't feel or think like he used to anymore, so I understood. His wife stood steadfast, kindly walking out life with him, and I thought, "Wow. Isn't this how we're supposed to be?" Whether in a marriage or relationship with a sibling or friend, you're not always going to say the right thing, and you're not always going to do the right thing.

LOVE WINS

However, in the end, if you allow love to always win, you can walk together with love winning in your heart for the other person. You can choose to see one another through love. You can forgive. Because if you don't let love win you will have bitterness, resentment and fear. Love prevents those things from remaining inside. Love allows you to have long-term relationships. Without love, you can't sustain any relationship with anybody. It does take boldness to be in relationship with someone for that long without walking away. It takes respect for them and it will take respect for you. It takes a willingness to take action. It takes a willingness to see that person as victorious no matter what. And it takes a lot of courage to remain in love when the world would want you to walk away from one another. Love requires strong intention.

BRAVERY IS LONG-TERM

I chose this story to begin this final week because bravery is a decision that will have long-term results. It takes courage for you to stay in relationship with yourself and with others. It takes bravery to be in relationship with someone you are married to, as well as someone you are simply friends with …

You exercise courage when you are in the midst of folks who may or may not celebrate you any longer. It takes you intentionally leading your pathway instead of your emotions leading you astray.

I want to encourage you to take this final week to heart and truly move forward into renewing who you are with a vision for whom you want to become.

LOVE YOURSELF LIST

This is BRAVE (Bold, Respectful, Activated, Victorious, Encouraging) week. Each day, I want you to take action for you and a friend. If you are in a small group, talk about what you all want to do in this next season of pressing forward. Set up a way to call each other. Make clear and concise goals on what you want to accomplish in the area of your worth. This list is jam-packed with each of you being kind to yourself and then extending that kindness to another person outside your group or sphere. Let's go.

- Accomplish something bold for yourself and then do something bold for someone else.
- Accomplish something that shows you respect yourself. Then do something that shows you respect someone else.
- Take action in an area you have been avoiding. Then take action to encourage someone else to take action. Let the domino of movement begin with you.
- Accomplish something that shows you are victorious over an area of your past. Then do something to help a friend be victorious over her past.
- Take action in an area that requires intentional courage. Be in courage. Then bring courage to someone else. This is more than encouraging you. This is stepping into an office — a position

of courage where you are making a stand. You are leading another person while you also move forward. You can do this! You are also encouraging a friend to do the same and follow your example.

DAY 36. A BOLD NEW ME

My Mind — The enemy between my own two ears has been defeated because Christ lives inside me. I am not all by myself. I am well able to take hold of my future because it will look nothing like my past.

My Mouth — I am bold. I am strong. I am confident. God is my Partner in Life and He is for me. Our future is bright.

My Move — I am writing down what I want to do today and in my tomorrows.

Reflection and Consideration

What do I have boldness in? What do I want to become? Am I dissatisfied deep inside? Can I pinpoint the specific issue? For example, do I hate poor treatment of the elderly, children or spouses? Do I hate injustice? Do I love to read the news and keep up on global reports? Today I choose to listen to my own heart and to look into my life.

I'm going to stop right now, look at the last number of years and consider what truly motivates me. I will find an important clue to what makes me the real me by reviewing my own personal life experiences.

> I am bold, and I am my own friend.

I have significance, and I am worthy. I will not shrink back from the real me or from what lives inside me. I do not have to have it all together, and I do not have to know exactly what I want. I will sit and consider if I have a long-lost dream. God is my Father and He wants to partner with me to bring me into my heart's true desires.

I want to think about my own value. I want to consider my own life and my own process. I want me to see myself as bold. I am well able to take action in areas that I have avoided. What do I want my future to look like?

God, I'm asking You right now. I will continue to ask. I will get still. I will be diligent. I will be consistent. I am going to be in Your face, Father. I am going to be like a little kid who is expectant to get something from her papa. Seriously. I am determined that You and I have a real relationship with authentic dialogue. You have a future for me, and You will lead me … into that future.

Summarizing 1 Samuel 17: David faced Goliath. David was aware of his own private strength and had already decided he was well able to conquer. In this confrontation with the giant, it was time for him to show his confidence in public.

You might want to read the history again. His actions will encourage you. David fought various battles in private, and then came the public confrontation with the giant. David was offended by Goliath's challenge to the armies of Israel. David refused to wear Saul's armor or clothing. He chose instead to approach the giant with a slingshot and stones from a nearby brook. David told the giant the Lord was going to deliver him into his hands. He also told him his plan to strike him down and cut off his head — all in the name of the God of the armies of Israel. David was bold. The bottom line is that David won the battle with the giant and was on his way to becoming the next king.

Spend time in thanksgiving and prayer. Picture yourself already bold, and imagine your victory.

What is my plan to show myself I am bold?

WRITE YOUR BOLD PLAN

DAY 37. A RESPECTFUL NEW ME

My Mind — I refuse to box myself into a corner filled with guilt and condemnation.

My Mouth — I am free to choose what is good and right for me.

My Move — How am I going to demonstrate respect for myself? How will I respect myself around the naysayers? How will I respond to those who affirm my change?

Reflection and Consideration

Donna's Story — Due to a bicycle accident, I had ugly teeth when I was a little kid. I also had abnormally large ears — at least the neighbor kept telling me I did, and I believed him. Although he was joking I always felt as if he was threatening to cut them off. He'd literally put a knife behind my ear and say, "I'm going to cut that off. It's so big." I dreaded going anywhere in public, and I hated myself. I hated the way I looked. I was afraid people were talking about me and thinking about how ugly I was. I was incredibly self-conscious, and I was full of low self-esteem. I had so little respect for myself. I didn't feel as if I was entitled to anything except shame. I didn't think I was entitled to anything except disrespect. I thought I deserved to be abused and hurt all the time. I felt I was destined to be the little-to-nothing person I felt like deep within.

I allowed myself to be abused. My thought was that eventually the ones who abused me would get around to loving me and liking me. That is how I allowed my thoughts to take on lies. My thinking was truly twisted. I figured as long as I let them hurt me, one day they might love me.

> I allowed abuse while I waited for other people to change.

Instead of choosing to change and disallow abuse, I waited for them to change. I really needed to see myself through different eyes. I allowed abuse. I invited people to shame me, accuse me, betray me and hurt me. I entertained it on purpose, thinking abuse was the only avenue to having others accept or love me.

Can you relate at all to my story? Perhaps you know someone who continuously allows himself or herself to be abused. What about you? Do you disrespect yourself? Maybe nobody sees it. Maybe nobody knows how you really feel about yourself. Maybe you hate yourself, and nobody knows. I'm asking you to truly and honestly look deep inside and ask yourself these questions: Do I like myself? Do I respect myself? Do I value myself? How you see yourself will show up in how you treat yourself. Possibly, people around you don't see your personal, private unbelief system. It is highly likely you live with a smokescreen and hide your pain.

Maybe you're some top-level executive. You go to work every day, and you're always popping out orders. Yet nobody really knows you. Each day you encounter yourself in the mirror. Each day you come home and are keenly aware of how you hid all day. Maybe you're a mom who continually, on the inside, can't stand the sight of yourself — but nobody knows. Listen. That's not the voice of a friend. That's not God's idea.

God made you beautiful, and He wants you to like and respect yourself. God has more respect for the human race than we show for one another. God is not a control freak. He made us in His image. He has great respect and value for us. The way He respects us is through His gift of free will. Think about how you have the free will to hate yourself, but it's not God's idea that you do. He wants you to respect you. He wants you to like you. He wants you to value you. He wants you to love you. We have been taking methodical steps over this season together so you can look at yourself from His perspective. It is legal to respect you. Look at you and realize where you lack this ability, and then make some changes. I want you to make changes to truly, truly, truly respect you in a new way this day, this week and this coming year.

Decision Making

What do you want your year to look like? What personal changes do you want to make in how you treat yourself?

> What exactly do you want to transform about yourself?

I want you to be concise in how you want to respect you and how you want others to respect you.

I want you to write this down. I want you to write down where you are not kind to yourself. And I want you to write down where you can change your mind. Are you like I used to be? Are you in the habit of allowing others to run you over, hunt you down and hurt you? Are you constantly asking what to do about this defeat and sabotage in your private world?

Let's switch gears. Maybe you run others down and you don't realize you treat others the way you feel about yourself. Perhaps you are unkind and short-tempered with those you love, because you feel unkind and short-tempered with yourself. Do you express your private feelings of despair by hurling anger toward those who love you enough to let you treat them unkindly? Do you express harsh feelings toward those who are powerless to stop you? These are difficult and gut level questions only you can answer. Honestly, the very respect you feel you do not receive from others might not be there because you do not respect them. What if what you demand is what you need to give?

I want you to write this down because we need to come to a solution of how to respect yourself. The perspective of God is you have value and worth. I want this to be your year to transition from whom you have been into whom God wants you to become ... someone who completely receives and accepts yourself as you are — with value, worth and respect.

> This is your time to pour kindness, love, mercy and compassion into yourself.

That's what I want this next season to be — a time of concentrating on your own private world. Let me also mention that you are not going to shut down and ignore your family, friends or responsibilities when you concentrate on you. You get to learn how to love yourself in the midst of your every day world living your life.

Spend time in thanksgiving and prayer. Picture yourself already bold, and imagine a deep respect within you for yourself.

What is my plan to show myself more respect?

WRITE YOUR RESPECT PLAN

DAY 38. AN ACTIVATED NEW ME

My Mind — I am unafraid to move forward.

My Mouth — I refuse to remain inactive in my greatest area of weakness.

My Move — What am I going to do?

Reflection and Consideration

What have you procrastinated in for so long that you are now afraid to take action? Do not allow fear to hold you any longer. I want to tell you something. I have been working on becoming a brave new me literally for years. I wrote out my thoughts and ideas for an actual book a thousand times. I miscarried ideas. I aborted thoughts of privately embracing a new me another thousand times. I started over and over countless times. Once I saw the solid idea for a book to help others, then I changed that book title and content a thousand times too. This idea of becoming new started close to seven years ago. That's how long I've been groaning and birthing this baby. I would take action, and then I would stop. Repeat. I was afraid to succeed. I was afraid to fail. So I would do nothing. I procrastinated. Why? I was birthing more than a book. I was birthing me.

I want to know if there is something inside you that you have needed to finish. What are you birthing?

> Are you in labor for your true self?

Do you have a long-standing area of private procrastination? Could breaking this habit be the key to finding who you are truly supposed to become? What if when you take action you find insight into your own career or personality? It could be the changes you make will give you opportunity to build character and welcome fresh relationships. Your actions may lead you to succeed in a public arena of society. As you take action and move forward into a specific area of fear, it might be your ticket to your own transformation. I want you to look at this area of procrastination. I want you to write it down and confront your own passivity and fears. I want you to truly consider how you can reform your own mountain of passivity.

I encourage you to read the **book of Esther** in the Bible, which is only a few chapters. The story goes like this: A young woman who had been living with her Uncle Mordecai became queen. A report about an attack directed toward the Jewish nation was leaked to her uncle. He had a heart for the people and challenged her to talk with her husband, the king. The problem was that in their culture, the wife was allowed to visit the king only when summoned. Mordecai challenged his niece to take a message to the king although it could cost her very life. She was deathly afraid. Yet he spoke to her fear and basically said, "Look, if you don't do it, somebody else will. Somebody else will rise up to the occasion. God is going to deliver His people." Esther did obey, and through a series of events, evil was exposed, and a plan to annihilate the Jewish people was terminated.

I want to encourage you today to live your life fully.

> You have a role to play in your own future.

Be your own Esther. Deliver yourself. Take the message to the King of Kings, and present your case before Him. He has already put the scepter in your court and said, "Yes. I want you to become. Yes. I give you permission to take action. Yes. It is time to become the new you. Yes. It is time to be successful. Yes. It is time to move forward. Yes. Yes. Yes." Because God is on your side, you can intentionally rise and decide to mature and live.

Today is your day to take action. This is your day. This is your week. This is your season. This is the time for you to get your own momentum. This is the time for you to take yourself out of transition.

Have you been in a holding pattern? Admittedly, waiting can sometimes be from God, but I think most of the time it is simply our own self-protection. Could it be we're the ones who lock ourselves in cycles and are afraid to take action? Are we afraid to take action? Are we afraid to fail? Are we afraid to move forward? Are we afraid to succeed or afraid to fail? Finally, are we afraid of what people are going to think about us?

I think we are afraid we're going to be embarrassed if we don't make it. We are afraid. If we run the race, what if we don't get first place, or what if we come in last place? It is ridiculous to remain so full of fear. It is time to take action and move out of those dread-filled belief systems. Let's transition out of how we have believed in the past and let's activate a brave new us.

Decision Making

So this is my challenge for you. Be your own deliverer. Take yourself out of transition. Present your case. Choose an area to take action in, and move into that area in your mind. Imagine yourself in that career role or already at peace instead of angry.

> What do you want to become?

Imagine it. The only ones who fail are the ones who quit. Do not quit. Just don't quit. Take action. It's time. Even if you pick up something that you tried to do 20 years ago — you know what? Take action. Make a plan, and give it a go! Give life your best shot, because you do not want to live in fear forever.

How do you want to be remembered? What do you want to be remembered for with your friends, family or society? You don't have to be famous. You know, you don't have to become someone who's known in books. You don't have to write the books either. But what if you are, and what if you do?

What if you have the next greatest invention? What if you are the one who comes up with something that solves a problem people have had for a long time, and God decides to bless your socks off financially? Listen, it's time to take action on the inside and the outside. Today is action day. This is action week for you to become the activated new you.

Spend time in thanksgiving and prayer. Picture yourself already activated. See yourself taking action in the areas you want to influence.

Start your plan of action.

WRITE YOUR ACTIVATED PLAN

DAY 39. A VICTORIOUS NEW ME

My Mind — I have pressed through.

My Mouth — I have not been overcome.

My Move — How am I going to demonstrate personal victory?

Reflection and Consideration

Where have you continued to fail over and over again in your past? Choose one area you want victory over. Maybe it's an area of your health. Maybe you simply have not been consistent in eating healthy or in physical exercise. Maybe it's in friendship or business. Perhaps it's in a schooling of some sort or a trade you're trying to learn. Possibly you've had the desire to read, and you just keep not reading. What if you want to learn how to cook in general or how to cook a different kind of dish? You could be single and lonely with minimal friends, yet deeply desire community. It could be you need to learn how to be your own friend in order to be a friend. Are you married and feel as though you are failing your spouse? Be practical, my friend.

> Maybe you just need to clean out your pantry or get a bottle of wine. Seriously.

Decision Making

Listen. I want you to choose an area you feel you are failing in, and I want you to make a plan to address it. I want you to write down what it is and what you think you need to do. Even if there are 100 steps, it doesn't matter. You may or may not know what it's going to take for you to accomplish your goal. So if you're a detailed person, write down all of the thoughts, ideas and action steps you need to take to move into victory over your passivity. This will help your brain.

Then I want you to decide what day you are going to start. And just do one thing at a time. Just one thing. Even if you accomplish only one step a week, do it. You can have victory in areas in which you have been defeated in the past. Therefore, I want you to choose an area in which you feel you have failed yet have decided you want victory.

I think it is wise to have short-term and long-term goals. Do something every week. If you take action every week, one year from today you will be closer to your goal than you are now. It's time to be victorious in old and new areas. It's time. You will see a difference in yourself, and you will notice that you are becoming a new you.

> Face Your Failure

One more thought in this area: Honestly, I'm the teacher who applauds all my students as long as they make effort. So this is my revelation: Whether or not you get your goal accomplished does not determine your success. True success is in facing your failure and facing those areas of weakness so you know (that you know) they no longer hold you captive.

I look forward to seeing you victorious over your past — because as you move forward, you will definitely become a brave new you.

Spend time in thanksgiving and prayer. Imagine victory. Imagine yourself already victorious over something in your past. See yourself already new.

Start your plan of victorious living.

WRITE YOUR VICTORIOUS PLAN

CHRIST IN YOU

YOU IN CHRIST

DAY 40. AN *IN-COURAGE* NEW ME

My Mind — I am my greatest encouragement. I am IN CHRIST and therefore *IN-COURAGE*.

My Mouth — I am *in courage,* and I am taking courage.

I AM BRAVE ...

I AM BOLDLY making new decisions.

I AM RESPECTING myself in new ways.

I AM ACTIVATED in life and moving forward.

I AM VICTORIOUS over my past.

I AM ENCOURAGING myself with *IN-COURAGE*.

My Move —What am I going to do to reflect courage inside me? I am getting out my mirror right now. I am facing myself in that mirror. I'm telling myself right now what I am about to do that is COURAGEOUS. Then I'm going to do it.

Reflection and Consideration

IN-COURAGE — I want you to look yourself in the mirror. I don't care if you're fat or tall, skinny or small, frail or strong. You must look at yourself and encourage yourself. What are you going to do in the name of *courage* in yourself and for yourself?

Are you waiting to be rescued? Maybe it is time to rescue yourself. Encourage yourself. You are worth it.

I want you to make declarations over yourself today. God created the world with His words. Can you create something with your words too?

> Create Your Own World

Let's continue to reinforce a victorious mindset:

I AM BOLDLY making the decisions to:

I AM RESPECTING myself by:

I AM now ACTIVATED in these areas:

I AM VICTORIOUS in this specific area of my past:

I AM consistently ENCOURAGING myself by:

Decision Making

God lives in you, and God breathes through you too. He also moves into you through the power of your own words. What will your words be? What do you want your words to bring forth in your future? What do you want your atmosphere to look today?

Tomorrow? Next week? Next year? Truly, you get to decide. You have the power.

> Be BRAVE

Say each one of these decrees with me:

I AM strong like a body builder.

I AM tall and sturdy like an oak tree.

I AM pure and cleansing like a waterfall.

I AM hot and purifying like the brightest sun breaking through clouds.

Now, my precious friend — I want you to read each one again, but now imagine yourself *as* the body builder, *as* the oak tree, *as* the waterfall and *as* the sun.

Spend time in thanksgiving and prayer. Picture yourself already courageous. Look in the mirror and see a lion looking back at you.

Write your own plan to step *IN-COURAGE*.

WRITE YOUR *IN-COURAGEMENT* PLAN

OUR TIME TOGETHER

I hope you have enjoyed *40 Days to the BRAVE New You*. I have enjoyed creating a new culture of honor for yourself. It surely stretched me. It empowered me. It challenged me in ways I did not know I needed to be challenged. It streamlined some areas in me I did not know needed to be addressed. It caused me to face weaknesses about myself I didn't know existed. Honestly, it really, truly birthed me into a new me ... and I hope it's done the same thing for you.

I want to encourage you to find some brave new friends. I'm not talking about ditching your current friends. I'm talking about inviting friends to enter into a fresh vision for their life. Maybe you have one friend you know could really find value in the transformation you have gone through.

Do you have friends who would enjoy and be challenged, encouraged and strengthened if they joined you in a *40 days to the BRAVE New You* study? I want you to consider leading a group into transformation. I believe in you!

I bless you today. This is the day to become a new person. This is the season. It's not too late. It's really not too late to reinvent yourself, and it's not too late to invite someone to go with you.

BRAVE NEW FRIENDS

It is time to celebrate your growth in esteem, love of God, friendship with God and friendship with yourself. Celebrate finishing if you did this study in a small group. If you had a partner, you can bring an appreciation gift to that friend for completing the race together. Let today be a day to celebrate progress, not perfection. Celebrate loving yourself.

You can even invite some friends to coffee or a small gathering at your house and introduce them to *40 Days to the BRAVE New You*. Would you like to facilitate a small group now that you have gone through the book? Contact me — I'm happy to help you help others love themselves.

Have you ever thought how amazing it would be if an entire city knew the Love of God? I would be honored to help you implement a vision bigger than yourself. Consider leading an entire city, region or community into Love.

Do you know five friends you feel would benefit from going through *40 Days to the BRAVE New You*?

Write their names here.

1.

2.

3.

4.

5.

Text, email or contact them via Facebook with information on how they too can go through *40 Days to the BRAVE New You* either with you or on their own. Feel free to give them my information, as I would love to encourage them.

SMALL GROUP ADVENTURE

After you have completed this study, I have some ideas on what you can do as a small group. First, I want all of you to take time and discuss your individual experiences. Talk about what you did to be bold, respectful, action taking, victorious over your past and encouraging for yourselves. Discuss how you got to know yourselves on a deeper level. I want your group to be real and have fun. The good stuff is next!

I want you to discuss what you all can do together as a group to enjoy each other and to build community. Here are some ideas for your group:

Plan a fun day at a beach.

Plan to run a race together.

Plan a dinner party together at a restaurant or someone's home.

Plan a weekend getaway together.

Plan needed meals for a friend in your group.

Plan to spring clean a friend's home in your group.

Plan to write out encouraging notes to one another for a specific amount of time.

Whatever you plan, I want you to thoroughly discuss this together. Be strategic and intentional. Be in agreement on the time frame, and remain focused while you follow through to bless and encourage.

While you plan, consider your steps. If you plan to have dinner together, plan ahead to financially bless the waiter or homeowner. You can pool together funds and provide childcare for parents.

As you get to know one another, you will be building community. You might discover a desperate situation within this small group that is private but needs immediate attention. Instead of an outside organization, this could also count as your small group assignment. Do whatever you agree to as a group. The challenge in growing is learning how to play well with others. In other words, can you come into a unified purpose just to bless someone else without getting exactly what you personally want? This is your chance to mature and learn how to love on an even deeper level.

I am BRAVER
#BEBRAVER

SMALL GROUP ASSIGNMENT

After you have had your own small group adventure, I want you all to discuss how you can benefit or bless another organization or group of individuals. How can you implement a strategy to impact them with boldness, respect, activation, victory or encouragement? As individuals, you have the opportunity to take action in unity as if you are one person.

I want you to discuss what you all can do together as a group to bless and encourage another community or organization. Here are some ideas for your group:

Gather clothes for a homeless shelter.

Plan a fundraiser to help a family meet medical needs or build a center to help trauma victims.

Purchase equipment to help teens or veterans learn a trade.

Provide a day of cake and punch for employees who work with troubled teens.

Bless the staff of a nursing home with balloons, cake and drinks.

Collect books to give to a home school co-op, nursing home, school library or at-risk youth program.

You can come up with a tangible way to bless another community. Once you have an idea, contact that organization and find out what steps are required to comply with their policies. It might seem like red tape but don't be discouraged — but press onward together. Then hand them the torch of encouraging someone else. Challenge them to go forward and bless others as a lifestyle.

BRAVE NEW YOU TAKEAWAY

These are my finals words to encourage you and love on you. This has really been a journey. This process has taken a long time — weeks and years, really — of looking at becoming a new person. I struggled to feel worthy initially. However, God is for me. My journey has included writing, erasing and starting over, again and again. The tension I felt in birthing myself brought out the best and worst of me. I got to learn how to embrace a new me. I have had a lot of bumps on the road. Friends have decided not to love me anymore. Friends have betrayed me. I have lived through odd and unusual misunderstandings, some of which never got resolved.

Much has happened in this long season of transformation. I've wept a river. I have poured out anguished, gut-wrenching crocodile tears with and for others. Recently someone we love and met with regularly passed away. He became a brave new him. He moved to Heaven. His spouse remains as she faces becoming a brave new her on planet earth. She is having to discover who she is without her partner of over 50 years. That's a strong place to have to embrace and move forward from.

I am confident you've had some challenges. And you have challenges ahead of you. I have challenges ahead of me. I just want to encourage you not to give up. I want you to know God loves you ... God truly sees you as the apple of His eye. I want you not to give in to the voices, thoughts and ideas that say you have no value or worth. You indeed have great value and great worth. You are made personally in the image of our Creator. You're unique. No matter what good you think about yourself, God thinks even better thoughts. He thinks higher thoughts. He thinks honoring thoughts. He thinks compassionate and life-giving thoughts. He sees you as He sees Himself.

I bless you. Thank you for coming on this journey with me. I would love to hear from you. I would love to hear your thoughts and ideas. I would love to hear things that came to your mind while you were going through the journey with me. I would love to know what was going on inside you. And I would love to know the changes that you implemented for yourself. I just want you to know I love you, and I thank you for walking this out with me. It's been a beautiful time.

PRAYING FOR YOU

God, I thank You for who You are. Father, I thank You for what You've done. God, I thank You for what it means — everything we understand and everything we don't understand. God, I thank You for resurrection. I pray that women will resurrect. I release resurrection.

SPEAKING TO YOU

I release you to rise. You have value and worth. You can rise up today. Rise in your environment. Rise and take authority over your atmosphere. Rise in your own home. Rise in your workplace. You can rise up in your relationships. You can rise up with your children. You can rise up in humanity. You can rise, because the Risen One lives inside you. I bless you today. I bless you with becoming your own brave new you.

RESOURCES AND THANK YOU

Thank you for participating in the *40 Days to the BRAVE New You* study. *It is a journey, really ... into the heart of Father God so a world can come to know His goodness in the land where they are living.* My prayer is that men and women rise in their understanding of their value and authority in their day-to-day living. I am interested in your opinion of this book. *In your letter, please include the organization or individual who referred you.*

You can find other books by Donna Reiners on Amazon.com. They include:
Woman, Come Out of the Cave
Becoming One
Voices in My Head
Talking Back to God

Woman, Come Out of the Cave is a Bible study. I've heard some women talk about the personal insight they received from me sharing my own life. After reading it, women have told me how they chose to live instead of killing themselves, how they were able to shake off mourning and grief, and how they learned to forgive family for deep, long-standing wounds. I'm real and raw regarding some circumstances in my past. It will strengthen you.

Becoming One is for women who want to be married or for married women who want more intimacy with the Lord or their husband.

Voices in My Head is a Bible study full of prayer and Scripture. It is like a conversational research tool with verses on the identity of Christ in you.

Talking Back to God (also offered in Spanish as *Respondiéndole a Dios*) is a Bible study that discusses who Jesus is, what He did and what it means for us. It talks about how, what, when and where Jesus prayed. It's not exhaustive, but it's pretty detailed on the prayer life of Jesus.

All intellectual property rights are owned by Donna and/or Craig Reiners. If you want to obtain inspirational materials or discover events by Donna Reiners, connect at DonnaReiners.com.

BIOGRAPHY

Donna Reiners is an author, speaker and life coach who lives in Katy, Texas with her husband Craig. They enjoy going to barbell strength classes and are learning how to eat and live healthy. They love relationship, not religion.

Follow her Facebook page: Donna Reiners author. Find her @donnareiners on Instagram and Twitter.

ENDNOTES

1. https://www.defensemedianetwork.com/stories/women-in-americas-world-war-ii-workforce/
2. Strong's Concordance number 1515
3. https://ig.ft.com/life-of-a-song/respect.html
4. I added part of the actual definition of the word *love* in that context from the Greek.
5. http://www.newadvent.org/cathen/08492a.htm#III Previous to this, according to Tertullian's testimony (De Praescript., xxvi), John had been thrown into a cauldron of boiling oil before the Porta Latina at Rome without suffering injury.

www.ingramcontent.com/pod-product-compliance
Lightning Source LLC
LaVergne TN
LVHW011812060526
838200LV00053B/3755